99 REASONS WHY NO ONE KNOWS WHEN CHRIST WILL RETURN

Foreword by
Hank Hanegraaff

B. J. OROPEZA

INTERVARSITY PRESS
DOWNERS GROVE, ILLINOIS 60515

InterVarsity Press® is the book-publishing division of InterVarsity Christian Fellowship®, a student movement active on campus at hundreds of universities, colleges and schools of nursing in the United States of America, and a member movement of the International Fellowship of Evangelical Students. For information about local and regional activities, write Public Relations Dept., InterVarsity Christian Fellowship, 6400 Schroeder Rd., P.O. Box 7895, Madison, WI 53707-7895.

All Scripture quotations, unless otherwise indicated, are taken from the HOLY BIBLE, NEW INTERNATIONAL VERSION®. NIV®. Copyright © 1973, 1978, 1984 by International Bible Society. Used by permission of Zondervan Publishing House. All rights reserved.

Cover photograph: J. A. Krauslis/Masterfile
ISBN 0-8308-1636-4

Printed in the United States of America ∞

Library of Congress Cataloging-in-Publication Data

Oropeza, B. J., 1961-
    99 reasons why no one knows when Christ will return/B.J.
Oropeza.
      p.   cm.
    Includes bibliographical references.
    ISBN 0-8308-1636-4
    1. Second Advent. 2. End of the world. I. Title. II. Title:
Ninety-nine reasons why no one knows when Christ will return.
BT886.0735   1994
236'.9—dc20   94-3576
                                          CIP

16	15	14	13	12	11	10	9	8	7	6	5	4	3	2	1
07	06	05	04	03	02	01	00	99	98	97	96	95	94		

Foreword

The prophet: John Hinkle
The platform: Trinity Broadcasting Network (TBN)
The prophecy: "The most cataclysmic experience that the world has ever known since the resurrection is going to happen."

Hinkle had his listeners' attention. He claimed that God, "in the most awesome voice," had told him, "On *Thursday, June the ninth,* I will rip the evil out of this world."

In his May 1994 newsletter, TBN president Paul Crouch elaborated on Hinkle's pronouncement. The voice, said Crouch, was "so *loud* and *clear* that it sounded like a great bell being rung by his ear!" Four days before the apocalyptic event was to take place, Hinkle, pastor of Christ Church Los Angeles (formerly Christ Church Unity), assured parishioners, "The glory of the Lord is coming upon everyone in this world in such a way they will see it outside, but ten thousand times more they will feel it inside."

As thousands waited anxiously for the great day to arrive, Crouch assured his vast television audience, "John has promised to be our special guest on June 9, 1994—that is, if we have not already been lifted to meet the Lord in the air."

Hinkle was a no-show on June 9. And so was the "cataclysmic experience."

Neither Crouch nor the pastor he had made famous apologized for the false prophecy. Instead, they employed a tactic that had worked for the Watchtower Society some eighty years earlier. Like the Jehovah's Witnesses who had predicted that Christ would return in 1914, they proclaimed that their prophecy had come to pass—only *invisibly.*

Crouch had already hedged his bets. On June 2 he declared, "Something may happen invisibly." For his part, Hinkle waited for June 9 to come and go. Then he sent his congregation the following communiqué: "At first myself and others were very disappointed it did not take place in the way we expected. It did begin, and is continuing to take place, but it happened in the spiritual realm first."

Prophetic pronouncements like Hinkle's are no longer rare. They've become all too common. A growing cacophony of voices now claim to have discovered the date of Christ's return.

☐ In *I Predict 2000 AD*, Lester Sumrall says the year is 2000: "I predict the absolute fullness of man's operation on planet Earth by the year 2000 AD. Then Jesus Christ shall reign from Jerusalem for 1000 years."

☐ Harold Camping predicted that Christ would return in September 1994. In his bestselling volume titled *1994?* he wrote, "When September 6, 1994 arrives, no one else can be saved, the end has come."

☐ Edgar Whisenant said Christ's Second Coming would occur in 1988. Millions fell for his Scripture-twisting tactics in the runaway bestseller *Eighty-eight Reasons Why the Rapture Will Be in 1988.*

As the year 2000 approaches, millennial madness continues to escalate, and an antidote is sorely needed. B. J. Oropeza's timely and trenchant book, *99 Reasons Why No One Knows When Christ Will Return*, provides just such an antidote. Not only does it put predictive prophecy into its proper perspective, but it also unmasks the biblical distortions of today's prophecy peddlers.

In clear and concise prose, Oropeza sounds the alarm against what he calls "cabala," "newspaper" and "comic-book" theologies.

Cabala theology might best be described as assigning secret, rather than sacred, interpretations to Scripture. For example, Harold Camping suggested that the two thousand demon-possessed pigs mentioned in Mark 5 actually represented two thousand years. He then added these two thousand years to the time of Christ's birth (which he believed to have been 7 B.C.) and came up with his prediction that Christ would return in 1994. But how did Camping know that the pigs represent years? This was his secret, personal interpretation.

Newspaper theology is focused on harmonizing items in the daily papers with the New Testament. One classic case involves a slew of ads placed by the Tara Center, a New Age organization, which proclaimed that the Christ—also known as Lord Maitreya— would soon reveal himself. Having seen the advertisement, a number of prophecy pundits immediately began proclaiming that Lord Maitreya was in fact the antichrist (some even took out their own ads to make the announcement). Not to be left behind, Huntington House Publishers published *New Age Messiah Identified* by self-proclaimed New Age expert Troy Lawrence. In the end the so-called Lord Maitreya turned out to be a hoax, as did Lawrence, who was exposed as a Mormon writing under an alias. Assigning absolute meanings to current events is dubious at best, and often dangerous.

Comic-book theology is equally damaging. Rather than focusing on the factual, it emphasizes the fanciful. Chick Publications, whose comic books and tracts permeate many Christian circles, provides a perfect example. In "Chick's World" there is never a shortage of conspiracies. The list of conspirators includes the pope, Kathryn Kuhlman and, of course, Christian Research Institute founder Walter Martin. Texe Marrs, another conspiracy theorist, not only impugns the credibility of longtime evangelist Billy Graham but adds Christian statesman Chuck Colson to a roster of individuals who are supposedly being used by the Vatican in its end-time global scheme. All of this is based on supposition and no evidence. Tragically, wild speculations like these are all too often circulated throughout the Christian community with reckless disregard for the reputations they destroy.

For all these reasons and more, Oropeza's call for Christians to abandon sensationalism and embrace the truth sounds a much-needed corrective note in today's world of discordant date-setters. While no one knows exactly *when* Christ will return, we do know that he *will* return. In the meantime we are called to be sober-minded and alert (1 Pet 1:13). Indeed, we should be prepared as though Christ were coming this very moment *and* prepared as though he may not come for yet another millennium.

Hank Hanegraaff
President, Christian Research Institute

Acknowledgments

I wish to give a special thanks to the volunteers and those on staff at the Christian Research Institute who assisted me with the research behind this project or critically evaluated portions of my manuscript. These people include Todd Gordon, Joan Moore, Ron Rhodes, Brad Sparks, Rich Abanes, Lynn Hammond and Erwin DeCastro.

I also wish to thank those who helped me with some of the resources behind this project or provided me with some other form of assistance. These people include Miriam Takahashi, Paul Carden, Rolly DeVore, Carol McElroy, William Alnor and Pastor Scott Temple.

1
Fascinated
by the
End Times

RAPTURE
OCTOBER 28, 1992
JESUS IS COMING IN
THE AIR

So read a full-page ad in the October 20, 1991 *USA Today*—one of many warnings financed by the frantic followers of yet another modern movement based on prophetic speculation. One fearful sect predicted that beginning on October 28, 1992, "50 million people will die in earthquakes, 50 million from collapsed buildings, 1.4 billion from World War III and 1.4 billion from a separate Armageddon."[1]

The source of the hysteria was the worldwide *Hyoo-go* (Rapture) movement, a loose collection of Korean sects mixing fanaticism, visions and end-time zeal. This movement is only one of many end-time predictors who have dogmatically affirmed the date of the rapture, when Christ returns to meet his church in the air.

Halfway around the globe from Korea, Hasidic Lubavitcher Jews from New York purchased Messiah beepers to know immediately when their grand rabbi, Menachem Mendel Schneerson, would be transformed into the Messiah. Another sect called the Ateret Hacohanim, convinced that their Messiah will rebuild the temple in Jerusalem at any moment, carefully study how to sacrifice animals according to the Law of Moses.

Secular soothsayers known as the Society for Secular Armageddonism established a voice-mail "Hotline of Doom." Residents of San Francisco can call (415) 673-DOOM to "hear warnings about nuclear and chemical weapons proliferation, toxic waste, deforestation, global warming, acid rain, increasing racism, AIDS, overpopulation, complacency and greed."[2]

Doomsday groups also cry out from the very pulpits of the evangelical church. Harold Camping, for instance, has written a bestseller published by Vantage Press entitled *1994?* in which he asserts: "If this study is accurate, and I believe with all my heart that it is, there will be no extensions of time. There will be no time for second guessing. When September 6, 1994, arrives, no one else can become saved, the end has come."[3] According to a spokesperson from the New York-based publisher, Camping's book had sold over fifty thousand copies by early 1993, and *Bookstore Journal* ranked it as the fourth bestselling prophecy book in February 1993.[4]

This intense zeal for future events will rise to a crescendo come the year 2000—the year that many believe will usher in the thousand-year reign of the Messiah on earth. Despite the fact that no one has ever been right about the day of the Lord's return, despite the biblical passages that argue against date-setting, despite the embarrassment Christians must face in the secular world every time a member of their camp sets a date that fails to materialize the Second Coming, doomsday fever persists.

In a 1993 survey conducted by *Time*/CNN, 20 percent of the adult population in America believed that Christ will return around the year 2000, and another 31 percent were not sure. More than 50 percent believed he will return sometime before A.D. 3000, and 22 percent believed a one-world government will rule the entire world during the next century.[5]

During the Persian Gulf conflict, a 1991 Gallup poll discovered that one out of every six Americans believed the U.S. war with Iraq would turn into the Battle of Armageddon. At the same time, prophecy books skyrocketed in sales. In just ten weeks John F. Walvoord's *Armageddon, Oil and the Middle East Crisis* sold 600,000 copies, and another 300,000 were distributed by Billy Graham.

But end-time speculation is nothing new. According to Christopher Columbus's *Book of Prophecies,* Columbus believed he was fulfilling prophecy through his explorations. He thought his calling was to lead a Christian army in the final crusade that would eventually convert the entire world to Christendom. His calculations led him to believe the world would end in 1656.[6] Columbus is just one of many forerunners of a current prophetic legacy—end-time date-setting.

Our Attitude Toward Prophecy

Why are we so fascinated by prophecy? There are at least three major reasons.

1. We all have a natural wish to know future events. Who hasn't at one time or another wanted to know how the world will end? The realm of the occult is full of fortunetellers, tarot and palm readers, astrologers and other soothsayers overtly attesting the reality of humankind's hunger for prophecy. As we approach the year 2000, I believe this tendency will increase. There is something foreboding about reaching a thousand-year marker. Only once in all of Christian history has this ever happened before.

2. Prophecy plays a prominent role in biblical revelation. Nearly one-fifth of the Bible is dedicated to prophetic writings, and the percentage is almost one-third for the Old Testament.[7] In the New Testament, Revelation is the longest book after Matthew, Luke, John and Acts. We cannot sweep such an enormous topic under the rug of doctrinal insignificance. Prophecy serves many functions, and one of them is to pronounce the coming Day of the Lord, when God will bring judgment on the kingdoms of humankind (Joel 1:15-16; 2:1-11; Zeph 1:2—2:3; 3:8-20; 1 Thess 5:1-3; 2 Thess 2:1-12; Rev 6:12-17; 16:13-21). In other words, prophecy *does* declare the end of the world as we know it.

3. A prophetic doomsday gives hope to those who have no hope. No one can avoid experiencing natural disasters, the death of loved ones, sickness, old age, crime, war and other calamities. Believing we have little or no control over these situations, we can easily feel help-less. At times the world can seem an awfully frightening place to live. According to one Barna Report, "Two-thirds of all adults believe 'the world is out of control these days' (64%). This perceived loss or lack of control has made the enjoyment of life even tougher for millions of adults."[8] Those who cannot see an optimistic future for our planet—or for their own lives—sometimes make sense of the foreboding future through prophecy. Christians can at least take comfort in the future's final outcome—Christ will prevail over Satan and destroy all earthly evil.

This is one reason I suspect Hal Lindsey's *The Late Great Planet Earth* became *the* bestseller of the 1970s. In the 1960s, Americans and others in the West experienced earth-shaking events that forever al-tered our foundations. With the Cuban missile crisis, John F. Ken-nedy's assassination, Vietnam, flower children, the Six-Day War and the first man on the moon, the 1960s transmogrified our 1950s Amer-ican dream into a nightmarish world of perpetual change. If we barely survived the 1960s, many wondered, what would happen during the 1970s? At this pivotal time Lindsey handed us a prophetic blueprint for the upcoming decades.

Before all of these apocalyptic events occur, Lindsey assured us, we would be taken away in the rapture to meet the Lord in the air. This was and still is the ultimate hope of many who see little hope for themselves or for the present world system. Those of us belonging to traditions that don't expect a pretribulation rapture—well, we are normally told that God will keep us safe through the calamities. Some Christians teach that entire societies will convert to Christianity, so future calamities do not pose much of a threat. They view the future more optimistically than most.

Our Attitude Toward the Future

Our hope for a better future in Christ raises some thorny questions. Is it right for a Christian to believe there is little or no hope for the world? Can't we make a difference in our community, country and world? If Christ sent out his disciples as lights in the midst of darkness, shouldn't we go out armed with the same attitude? The end is on its way, no doubt, but this should not be taken as an incentive to sit back and revel in prophecy speculations.

Some get so obsessed playing the puzzle-game of prophecy that they forget a prophetic parable that they may themselves be fulfilling. As he prepared to leave on a long journey, a master gave each of his stewards a talent to work with until he returned. One steward buried his talent instead of using it for the master's purposes. When the master returned, this steward was punished (Mt 25:14-30). Have some of us, convinced that the world will end in our lifetime, become so heavenbound that we are no earthly good?

Others catch an evangelistic zeal once they think they know the date of Christ's return, but their evangelism usually amounts to nothing more than passing out material promoting their Second Coming forecast. Once their date fails, so does the credibility of their message.

Still others who lack discernment are continually duped by date-setters. In the 1980s, 4.5 million copies of Edgar C. Whisenant's *Eighty-eight Reasons Why the Rapture Will Be in 1988* were distributed worldwide. After that prediction failed, Whisenant said he had accidentally miscalculated his date, and he sold thousands of more copies of *The Final Shout: Rapture Report 1989*. He has reprinted this book every year since then, changing the date as each new year arrives.

Those of us who knew better watched as Whisenant's 1988 omen passed without bearing fruit. We dismissed him as mistaken, but we never bothered addressing his arguments. Knowing that it makes no sense to try to set dates, we usually respond to date-setters with the comment, "Well, let's wait and see if your prophecy comes to pass." But the kinds of arguments Whisenant uses are being picked up and repackaged by other date-setters, creating a vicious cycle. Many new dates keep surfacing because we've failed to unearth the root of all date-setting—*faulty biblical interpretations and dogmatic speculations about current events.*

How This Book Addresses Prophecy

Chapters two through five of this book examine Bible passages that are often distorted by date-setters. In chapters six and seven I respond to those who dogmatically connect current world events with biblical prophecy. Chapters eight and nine answer date-setting arguments derived from nonbiblical sources, while chapters ten through twelve address miscellaneous issues such as end-time rumors and attempts to name the antichrist and decode the mark of the Beast. The final two chapters stress the dangers behind date-setting and discuss four things we *can* know about the end times.

This book, then, has a twofold purpose. It is written to discourage Christians from setting or suggesting dates for Jesus' return and from being dogmatic about tying prophecy to current events, trends and persons. Writers and teachers who make these mistakes range from cult leaders to respected evangelicals. Please note: I am not claiming that the evangelical teachers listed in this book are cultic, unorthodox or false prophets. Many are dedicated Christians who love the Lord but have overstepped their prophetic boundaries through date-setting or dogmatic speculating. I pray they will accept this reproof as constructive criticism (Prov 9:8-9; 27:5-6).

On a more positive note, I hope that the reader who studies this book will gain tools to recognize the misinformation perpetrated by those who set end-time dates. And I believe the careful reader will be able to correct others who have been confused by such teaching.

This work is not an exhaustive genealogy of who's who in date-setting, nor is it a point-by-point refutation of every single argument ever espoused by prophecy buffs. It does, however, sample the teachings of some of the major players. It also addresses the most difficult arguments they raise and gives reasons—ninety-nine in all—why no one knows when the Lord will return.

2
Reasons Why
No One
<u>Knows the Date</u>
<u>Through</u>
<u>Scripture</u>

*H*e claimed to be the messianic Joshua prophesied in the book
of Zechariah. His calling was to prepare the bride of Christ
for the rapture and to convert Israel to Christianity. His
followers saw him as a dynamic preacher and miracle-worker. Sometimes he would lose his temper and throw microphones at church
members. He prophesied that the houses of his enemies would burn
down; he hoped his followers would fulfill this vision. He confessed
to committing adultery in his congregation. Many thought he would
eventually poison his followers.

Jim Jones? Yes and no. His name *is* Jim Jones, but he is not the
Jim Jones who headed the People's Temple in Jonestown, Guyana,
and in 1978 led 912 followers in a mass suicide. Instead, this Jim Jones
presides over the Spoken Word Tabernacle in the small town of Camp

Verde, Arizona. A Yava County grand jury charged him with two counts of molestation involving teenage girls in his congregation. Jones believed he would be vindicated, however, for God allegedly told him that on December 25, 1992, he would be set free from "Egypt" (the world). Mario Chagolla, a former deacon of the church, said, "If he's getting closer to the date of his trial and believing [in his day of vindication] with all his heart, he's going to possibly poison the people. . . . That's the rapture."[1]

The Reverend Jim Jones cannot be Joshua or the messianic "Branch" (Zech 3:8; 6:11-13). The "Branch" prophecies, references to the coming Messiah who would be linked to the line of King David, were fulfilled in the first coming of Christ (Is 11:1-5; Jer 23:5-6; compare Rev 22:16). Yet the Reverend Jones is not alone in his biblical interpretations. Many other ministers distort the Word of God in order to justify their date for the rapture or the Second Coming.

This chapter examines the biblical passages most often misinterpreted by date-setters. Here's a list of reasons why no one knows the time of Christ's return through Scripture.

Reason 1: Scripture Does Not Give Us a Specific Date for the End Times

When my doorbell rang, I opened the door to meet two women who said they were from the Watchtower Bible and Tract Society. One of the first questions they asked was whether I believed we were living in the last days. I told them yes (even though I knew my interpretation of "last days" contradicted theirs). Our conversation then gravitated toward 1914, when, according to Jehovah's Witnesses, the Second Coming took place. Christ returned that year, but no one could see him because his return was invisible.

I asked the elder of the two women, "What objectively happened in 1914 that should make everyone believe Jesus Christ returned?"

She failed to give me a direct answer. She only affirmed that we are living in the last days according to Scripture and that therefore Jesus Christ returned in 1914.

The Bible never gives a date for the return of Christ. The Jehovah's Witnesses could offer no biblical proof text even from their own distorted New World translation—there is no text that says, "Jesus will return in A.D. 1914." In general, date-setters must go beyond any plain reading of Scripture in the attempt to unearth some hidden date for the Lord's return.

Many date-setters assign biblical passages a *spiritual* meaning whenever the literal one doesn't suit their purposes. Thus they renew an error that was widely perpetrated in the Middle Ages: the assumption that the average layperson cannot properly understand Scripture. Since most of us are incapable of mining biblical secrets, the date-setter feels called to provide that hidden message about when the end will take place. And usually the date-setter's followers are the only people who can track with the date-setter's unusual logic in the interpretation of Scripture.

The Watchtower is the only "faithful and discreet slave" dispensing biblical truths, according to the Jehovah's Witnesses' interpretation of Matthew 24:45-46. But who told them the Watchtower was this slave? The Watchtower did! Thus Jehovah's Witnesses must believe the Watchtower is God's only true prophet not because Scripture says so, but because their organization says so.

The Watchtower originally believed that Christ returned invisibly in 1874. Then its founder, Charles Taze Russell, predicted the rapture in 1910, with the end of the world occurring in 1914. Long after the doomsday date failed, the Watchtower once again revised its doctrine by moving Christ's invisible return from 1874 to 1914.[2]

The Watchtower also claimed that those living in 1914 were the final generation. According to its literature (based on Psalm 90:10) a generation lasts seventy to eighty years.[3] Now that eighty years have transpired since 1914—and almost every Watchtower witness who lived during that era is either dead or very old—the society will have to change its date once again.

The Lord's return in 1914 is not supported by Scripture. What we do find in Scripture is that false prophets like those of the Watchtower Society claim that Christ has returned secretly (Mt 24:23-28).

Reason 2: Jesus Will Come like a Thief in the Night for Both Believers and Nonbelievers

"Therefore keep watch, because you do not know on what day your Lord will come. But understand this: If the owner of the house had known at what time of night the thief was coming, he would have kept watch and would not have let his house be broken into. So you also must be ready, because the Son of Man will come at an hour when you do not expect him" (Mt 24:42-44). The Lord's coming will be like that of a thief in the night, according to this Matthew passage, 1 Thessalonians 5:1-2, 2 Peter 3:10 and other passages.

Turning these passages on their head, Edgar Whisenant highlighted 1 Thessalonians 5:4: "But you, brothers, are not in darkness so that this day should surprise you like a thief." In Whisenant's view, "This means that the wicked will be surprised, but the faithful will not be surprised at the Rapture. . . . If the Rapture is supposed to be a surprise, you cannot see the day approaching [Heb 10:25]."[4]

It is true that Jesus will come back like a thief for those who are not ready. In other words, he will come *unexpectedly* and they will be caught in their sins (Mt 24:45-51; 1 Thess 5:3-11). Yet he will also come unexpectedly even to those who *are* ready—the difference is that they will be prepared to meet him, since they have kept themselves pure. Those who are "of the night" (living in sin) will be taken by surprise (1 Thess 5:4-11; compare Rom 13:11-14). But those who are "of the day" walk in faith, obedience and self-control. They will not be surprised by the suddenness of Christ's return. The only New Testament occurrences of the word *sudden (aiphnidios)* are in 1 Thessalonians 5:3 and Luke 21:34; in both instances it describes Christ's unexpected coming.

As a whole, 1 Thessalonians urges us to be prepared for the end by virtue of godly conduct, not by a knowledge of when Christ will return (1:9-10; 3:13; 5:23). In fact, most New Testament references to the rapture or the Second Coming of Christ admonish Christians to live righteously, but no reference ever tells us to find out the date of his return (see, for example, Lk 12:35-46; 1 Cor 1:7-8; Col 3:1-10; 1 Pet 1:13; 4:7; 2 Pet 3:10-12; 1 Jn 2:28-29). Jesus is speaking specifically to his followers when he says, "So *you* also must be ready, because the Son of Man will come at an hour *when you do not expect him"* (Mt 24:44; compare Mk 13:33-37).

Paul writes, "Now, brothers, about times and dates we do not need to write to you, for you know very well that *the day of the Lord* will come like a thief in the night" (1 Thess 5:1-2). Jesus used the same words when telling his disciples that they could not know the "times or dates" of the end (Acts 1:7). Through this teaching handed down by the apostles, the Thessalonians already knew that no one could know when the end would take place. Paul is simply reaffirming the "thief in the night" teaching of Christ (Mt 24:36-51); that is why he says, "About times and dates we do not need to write to you." The Day of the Lord (which in this context includes the rapture; 1 Thess 4:13—5:11) would overtake *all* like a thief in the night, but as long as the Thessalonians were living godly lives they had nothing to fear.

Reason 3: The Call to Watch for the Lord's Coming Does Not Mean We Will Know the Date

Date-setters commonly peddle Scriptures telling us to "watch" for the Lord's coming. In Matthew 25:1-13, believers are to watch so they will not be excluded from the marriage of the Lamb as were the five foolish virgins. Revelation 3:3 states: "But if you do not wake up, I will come like a thief, and you will not know at what time I will come to you." Marilyn J. Agee, an author who teaches that the rapture will take place in 1998, comments thus on this verse:

What an astonishing statement. Do you realize what it implies? Reread it and think about it. A secret is hidden there. If we do not watch, we will not know when Christ will come upon us. But, what will we know if we do watch? Startling isn't it? Inherent in Jesus' declaration is the reverse, that if we do watch, we will know when he will come upon us.[5]

What do we make of passages telling us to watch for Christ's return? Let's look at them closely.

Revelation 3:3: Should the watchman cry wolf? Revelation 3:3 was originally written to the church of Sardis. The word *watch* (*grēgoreō* in Greek) can also be translated "awake," "wake up" or "be alert" (see the New American Standard and New International versions). The church in Sardis has spiritually fallen asleep (3:1). The Lord exhorts them to wake up from their slumber and strengthen what is still alive in their midst (3:2). If they continue to doze, they will not be ready for the Lord's visitation. The Sardis believers need to be spiritually awake—in other words, living godly and fruitful lives. They should not be spiritually asleep (compare Rom 13:11-14; 1 Thess 5:5-11).

This passage does not mean that those who watch for end-time signs will know the date of the Lord's return. Rather, those who are spiritually alert and prepared will be ready for the Lord *whenever* he returns (see Mk 13:32-37).

This warning carried a special significance for the people of Sardis. At least twice in its history Sardis had been subdued by enemy forces (by Cyrus of Persia in 549 B.C. and by Antiochus the Great in 216 B.C.) because the city's defenders had failed to be watchful. In ancient times, if an enemy attacked a city when the watchmen were not occupying their assigned post or were distracted or had fallen asleep, the watchmen had failed. It was not the watchman's duty to predict the date of the enemy's arrival. His job was to alert the city to prepare for an attack when the enemy was already visible. If the watchman sounded an alarm when he anticipated an enemy's arrival but had not actually seen the enemy, he would not be a watchman very long!

Similarly, Christians are to watch for the Lord's coming by keeping spiritually alert and prepared, not by predicting the time frame of his arrival. Those who cry wolf with no doomsday in sight soon lose their credibility.

And we need to consider a further point as we look at Revelation 3:3. Most scholars affirm that the judgment referred to here is not necessarily the rapture or Second Coming. Here the foretold judgment is probably either Roman or (later) Muslim persecution. Revelation 1:1—3:22 refers to events that are "now" (1:19)—in other words, contemporary to John's time—while the events that "will take place later" (1:19; 4:1) are covered in Revelation 4:1—22:21. The warnings of impending judgment in Revelation 2:1—3:22 most likely predict the early persecutions that, from our perspective, have already taken place hundreds of years ago.[6]

Matthew 25:1-13: Watch or prepare? Does the parable of the ten virgins (Mt 25:1-13) really teach us to seek to know the timing of the end so that we will not be left behind? Remember that the passage just before this, Matthew 24, teaches that no one knows the time of the Lord's return. In the parable at the end of that chapter, the wise servant was prepared through godly living and the foolish unprepared because of ungodly living (24:45-51).

Jesus reinforces this same point in the parable of the ten virgins. The wise virgins were prepared and the foolish unprepared to meet their lord. Far from being date-setters, *both* the wise and the foolish virgins fell asleep (Mt 25:5). Obviously, none of them knew in advance when the bridegroom would come. But since the wise—anticipating a long wait—had brought along extra oil for their lamps, they were prepared for the bridegroom's arrival (25:1-4).

Suddenly at midnight, "the cry rang out: 'Here's the bridegroom! Come out to meet him!' " (25:6). This does not prove that right before the end we will suddenly know the time of the Lord's return. The time to prepare was *before* the cry. The wise virgins were ready even before they were aware of the bridegroom's arrival. And the foolish virgins were punished not because they didn't know the time of the bridegroom's return but because they did not bring extra oil—meaning that they were not spiritually prepared to meet him. The parable once again emphasizes that we will not know the time of the Lord's return (25:13).

Reason 4: God Has Not Given Us All the Specific Details About the End Times

James was troubled. He had just encountered a zealous man preaching that the rapture would happen on October 28, 1992. James, a student of mine, was not a gullible person. He knew this soothsayer was wrong and told him so. The date-setter responded with Amos 3:7: "Surely the Sovereign LORD does nothing without revealing his plan to his servants the prophets." James, stunned, hadn't known how to reply.

On the surface this verse appears quite convincing, especially when coupled with Jesus' words "For there is nothing hidden that will not be disclosed, and nothing concealed that will not be known or brought out into the open" (Lk 8:17; compare Mt 10:26-27; Mk 4:22). Guatemalan pastor Marvin Byers, who teaches that the rapture will happen in the year 2000, writes, "Therefore, if we do not understand the last days, we lack understanding of at least one-third of the Bible! The Spirit of Truth desires to lead us into truth in this area also [John 16:13]! . . . Every detail will be revealed to someone! He will do *nothing* without first sharing His secret with his friends!"[7]

A closer look at the Scriptures exposes this typical error made by date-setters. God already *has* revealed his future plan to us in the book of Revelation. He has not kept secret what he will do in the future. But he has kept from us any *further* revelation regarding the events described in Revelation—those who "add anything" to the revelation are threatened with exclusion from his kingdom (Rev 22:18-19).

In Amos 3:7 the word *plan,* or in some versions *secret* (*sôd* in Hebrew), does not mean that every detail must be revealed. Although God predicted the destruction of Samaria by Assyria (Amos 3:8-15), he never gave Amos a specific date for this destruction. Even in the book of Revelation God refuses to disclose the message of the seven thunders (10:3-4). So God has already given us all that we need to know about the future, but he does not give us every detail—such as the date of the rapture (Deut 29:29; Eccles 3:11; Mt 24:36).

God didn't even reveal all future details to the prophets whose writings are included in the Bible (see Dan 12:8-9; 1 Pet 1:10-11). In Amos 3:7-15 God does not reveal to Amos the name of the "enemy" or the exact date of this particular day of judgment (3:11, 14).

If God reveals every detail before it happens, then why didn't he reveal the date of the Jews' 1948 return to Palestine, the date of the Six-Day War in Jerusalem, the date of the fall of communism in Russia and so forth? Virtually all doomsday-setters consider such events prophetically significant, yet we have no evidence that anyone predicted the date—not even the month or year—of these events before they occurred.

In Luke 8:17 and related passages, that which was hidden and would one day be revealed was the teachings Jesus privately gave his disciples (see, for example, Mt 16:20; Mk 4:10-12, 33-34; 9:9). All of these teachings would be declared abroad once Jesus was risen from the dead (Lk 8:16). In these passages Jesus is not making any promise to reveal new information about the date of the end times.

What about John 16:13—doesn't the Holy Spirit reveal things to come? He certainly does, but as is clear in the context of John 14 through 16—one long message of comfort that Jesus gave to the apostles before he was betrayed—Jesus is giving this promise *only* to his apostles (compare John 14:16-26; 15:26-27; 16:7-13). "What is yet to come" most likely refers to the new Christian order which was still in the apostles' future. After all, Christ had not yet been crucified. If this promise does have any application after the formation of Christianity, the Spirit would give further revelation to the apostles to complete the New Testament. The revelation already given to us through Scripture is entirely sufficient for our life in Christ, and no date for the Lord's return needs to be added to it. So John 16:13 does not indicate that the Holy Spirit will reveal to us the date of prophetic events.

Reason 5: Examples from the Old Testament Are Insufficient to Warrant Date-Setting

The Old Testament is an amazing book. It foretells the first coming of Jesus in many places (for example, Ps 22; Is 53; Dan 9). Noah predicted the end of the preflood world in Genesis 6. God revealed to Abraham his imminent destruction of Sodom and Gomorrah (Gen 18:17—19:27).

Unfortunately, some people use such Old Testament passages as proof texts to justify date-setting. They reason that since God revealed future events in the Old Testament—sometimes even setting dates— New Testament believers are granted this same privilege. Harold Camping, the founder of Family Radio and Open Forum, sees himself as a modern-day Jonah.[8] As Jonah prophesied that in forty days Nineveh would fall (Jonah 3:4-9), so Camping predicted that the world would be destroyed in September 1994.

The Old Testament was written before the entire prophetic picture was revealed in the New Testament. Hence to use Old Testament examples to justify date-setting is to commit an error known as the *fallacy of anachronism:* projecting the realities of one era into a different time where different conditions prevail. For instance, it would be wrong for us to revert to the Old Testament practice of sacrificing animals for our sins. Why? Because according to the New Testament, Christ became the final sacrifice for our sins on the cross. If we still sacrificed animals, this would indicate that we do not really believe Christ's death sufficiently covers our sins.

Similarly, God may have revealed certain dates to Old Testament prophets, but this does not mean he will do so for us. Why not? Because he has already determined not to reveal any more future dates to New Testament believers (Mt 24:36; Acts 1:7; 2 Thess 2:1-4). If God wanted us to know the date of the end, he would have given us that date back in the first century through the apostles. As noted in reason 1, no such date is offered in Scripture. Those who allegedly find one must twist the Word of God to get it (2 Pet 3:16).

Reason 6: We Have Been Living in the Last Days for Almost Two Thousand Years

Often Christians are told they are living in the last days. This is true, but it is not unique to our time. We have been living in the "last days" since the first century (Acts 2:17-23; 1 Cor 7:26, 29; 10:11; Phil 4:5; Heb 1:2; 2 Pet 3:3-4; 1 Jn 2:18; Rev 1:1-3). The early Christians believed in the imminence of Christ's return just as many Christians do today. Their conception of the last days, however, may differ from that of many of today's prophecy advocates. First-century Jews and Christians divided history into the following major eras:

How Jews Viewed History

Before creation	Between creation and the coming of the Messiah	After the coming of the Messiah

How Early Christians Viewed History

Before creation	Between creation and the coming of Christ	Between Christ's first and second comings	After Christ's second coming

The early Christians, who adapted the Jewish model of time, believed that the first coming of the Messiah occurred in the first century. They themselves were past the midpoint of history; hence they were living in the last days.

One theologian writes, "It is already the time of the end, and yet is not *the* end. This tension finds expression in the entire theology of Primitive Christianity. The present period of the Church is the time between the decisive battle, which has already occurred, and the 'Victory Day.' "[9] We sometimes fail to recognize that the kingdom of God has already been established on earth (Mt 13). What we are awaiting is its full realization, the Victory Day that will occur at Christ's Second

Coming. Meanwhile, we live in a paradoxical age of "now but not yet." As was the case with the first-century saints, the fact that we live in "the last days" does not necessarily mean that Christ will return in our lifetime.

Reason 7: Daniel's Prophecy of Seventy Weeks Does Not Give Us a Date for the End

According to Marvin Byers, Daniel 9:24-27 gives us the date of the rapture. Daniel 9:25 speaks of seven weeks of years (each day represents a year, so one week equals seven years), or forty-nine years (7 × 7), and then of sixty-two weeks of years, or 434 years (7 × 62), from the time of the rebuilding of Jerusalem until the Messiah. Byers claims that the rebuilding of Jerusalem began in 445 B.C., when King Artaxerxes sent Nehemiah to rebuild the walls of Jerusalem (Neh 2). Adding 434 years to this date, we arrive at 11 B.C.

Byers then adds twenty-three hundred days, based on Daniel 8:13-14. In the second century B.C. the tyrant Antiochus Epiphanes persecuted the Jews for twenty-three hundred days, and Jewish sacrifices were abolished in the temple. These days are attached to his calculation because "the Seventy Weeks are in progress only while Israel is governed from within."[10] The twenty-three hundred days (about six years and four months) are added to 11 B.C. to bring us to 5 B.C., the year of Christ's birth.[11]

Yet this leaves forty-nine years from Daniel 9:25 unaccounted for. These years, Byers asserts, should be calculated from the new rebuilding of Jerusalem that began in November 1947. When we add forty-nine years to this date, we can know that the Messiah will return around September 1996! On this date Christ will be "birthed" in his church, demonstrating the power of his kingdom. But it isn't until three and a half years later (based on the last half of Daniel's final seventieth week in Daniel 9:27) that Christ will rapture his church.[12]

There are several flaws in Byers's proposal.

First, the order of weeks is out of sequence. There is no sufficient reason that the angel Gabriel would confuse Daniel on this already extremely difficult topic by switching the time segments. In Daniel 9 the seven weeks (forty-nine years) come *before* the sixty-two weeks (434 years). So 7 and 62 should be added together to become sixty-nine weeks of years, or 490 years. The date for the commencement of this prophecy is most likely 457 B.C., when Artaxerxes I had Ezra rebuild Jerusalem (Ezra 7:1-26; 9:9). The seven weeks (forty-nine years) of Daniel 9:24, then, refers to the time when the rebuilding of the city would be *finished* (Dan 9:25). That occurred about 408 B.C. If we now add the sixty-two weeks of years (434), we arrive at the beginning of Jesus' ministry in A.D. 27. The forty-nine years of Daniel 9:24, then, have nothing to do with the year 1947. So what happened to Daniel's final, seventieth week?

Some may assert that this final week represents the entire church era. According to some scholars, the chronology in Daniel 9 should not be interpreted literally. They claim that the number 70 merely represents completion, indicating the completion of the work of redemption in humankind at the Second Coming of Christ (see Dan 9:24). Other scholars believe that the final week (seven years), or at least the last half of the final week (three and a half years), represents the period of the Great Tribulation, which is still in our future (Rev 11—19). Although either seven or three and a half years might be the actual length of the final tribulation, Daniel's seventieth week does not tell us *when* the Great Tribulation will take place.

Second, there is no good explanation why the years of Jesus (from his birth to the beginning of his ministry thirty years later) are excluded from the calculation. Daniel 9:26 says that after sixty-two weeks the Messiah would be "cut off." Byers claims that Christ was being "cut off" right after he was born. He first started suffering when he was circumcised as an infant![13] But the passage does not warrant such an interpretation. The cutting off of the Messiah refers to his crucifixion, a once-and-for-all event (Is 53:8). The Hebrew word for "cut off" *(yikkarēṯ)* is in the future tense. When applied to humans, this word virtually always implies punishment by death (as in Gen 9:11; Lev 17:14; Num 15:31; Obad 9; Zech 13:8). The Messiah was put to death 490 years from the rebuilding of Jerusalem. Had Daniel wished to portray the Messiah's circumcision, we would assume he would have used a variant of the Hebrew word *mûl,* meaning "to cut off, or circumcise" (Gen 17:23; 21:4).

Third, and most important, date-setting from Daniel's seventieth week violates Scripture's clear affirmations that no one knows the time of the Lord's return (Mk 13:32; Acts 1:7). Like other Scriptures, Jesus' words "No one knows the time" will not pass away until heaven and earth pass away (Mk 13:31). So there can be no future time when someone will know the date of the end—until the end actually comes.

Finally, there is no evidence that the twenty-three hundred days of Daniel 8:14 should be excluded from the seventy-week calculation. Byers claims that the seventy weeks include only periods when Israel is running its own affairs. If this were true, then Byers should exclude the many years when the Jews were under a foreign power in Jerusalem. Such were the times of Bagoses, Ptolemy Soter and Pompey (Josephus *Antiquities* 11.297; 12.1; *Wars* 1.141). Each of these rulers brought Jerusalem under his power within the 490-year time frame of Daniel's seventy weeks.

In any case, there's a better explanation for the twenty-three hundred "days." You'll read about it in the discussion of reason 8.

Reason 8: Daniel's Twenty-three Hundred Evenings and Mornings Do Not Give Us a Date for the End

"No book ever written is as audacious or bold as one that claims to predict the timing of the end of the world, and that is precisely what this book presumes to do."[14] So begins Harold Camping's bestseller *1994?* Camping believed the final tribulation (which he claims started on May 21, 1988) would last till September 6, 1994 (the day of the Jewish Feast of Trumpets), and then Christ would return sometime between September 15 (the Day of Atonement) and September 27, 1994 (the last day of the Feast of Tabernacles):

To summarize, if we are on the right track, we would expect the year 1988, which is the 13,000th anniversary of the world, to begin the final tribulation spoken of in Matthew 24:15-29. We know from Daniel 8 that the final tribulation period will be 2300 days, which is six years. Therefore, six years later than 1988 (actually 2300 days), Christ would return and we would be at the end of this world's existence. That is the year 1994.[15]

Do the twenty-three hundred days of Daniel 8:14 give us the length of the Great Tribulation? Actually, Daniel 8:14 speaks of twenty-three hundred "evenings and mornings." This refers to the suspension of the temple sacrifices, which were offered every evening and morning (see Ex 29:42). Thus the twenty-three hundred days should be divided in two, making a total of 1,150 days (roughly three years and fifty-five days). Historically, this time span corresponds to the desecration of the temple in Jerusalem by Antiochus Epiphanes, the Seleucid king whose kingdom is represented as one of the four horns in Daniel 8:22-26.

History tells us that Antiochus's administrators apparently forbade any temple offerings in the Jewish month of Tishri (September-October) in 167 B.C. and that they set up an abominable idol in the temple one and a half months later. The sacrifices were not begun again until the rededicating of the temple under the leadership of Judas Maccabeus in 164 B.C., on day 25 of the month Chislev (1 Maccabees 1:20-59; Josephus *Antiquities* 12.7.6-7).[16] The temple rededication occurred 1,150 days after the sacrifices were first banned.[17]

Camping took a prophecy already fulfilled in history and converted it into the length of the final tribulation. He also mistakenly doubled the time period alluded to in Daniel 8:14.

Reason 9: Discerning the Signs of the Times Does Not Warrant Date Suggestions

David and Michele recently wrote: "Our friend and several of her friends are now trying to liquidate their assets and buy land in the country, to live on and grow food on, in the event of a crisis. I see their actions as rather extreme (a form of 'Millennial Madness,' if you will)."[18] Who influenced David and Michele's friend to retreat from the city? Not a cult leader but, sadly enough, a popular evangelical minister by the name of Jack Van Impe.

Mesmerized by Van Impe's authoritative predictions that the European Economic Community would officially unite in 1993, combined with some strange calculations allegedly pointing to Christ's return in A.D. 2000, David and Michele's friend was convinced the end was at hand. Yet Van Impe agrees that no one can know the day or hour of the Lord's return. He does not believe in date-setting, but still he claims the signs are so clear that we can know Jesus' coming is right around the corner.[19] Van Impe is involved in the dangerous game of date-*suggesting*.

Even Hal Lindsey, back in the 1970s, had us believing that our generation would not pass away until all the end-time signs were fulfilled (Mt 24:32-34). In his estimation, forty years was the length of a generation—so the Lord *might* return by 1988. "The decade of the 1980s," Lindsey suggested, "could very well be the last decade of history as we know it."[20] Mere speculation? Some would think so.

No doubt Lindsey's books have been used by God to reach many unbelievers, but does this vindicate his date-suggestions? I think it is reasonable to assume that God has blessed Lindsey's books *in spite* of his speculations. Lindsey has since apologized for overstating his original predictions, but he still believes we are living in the final generation.

Had I seriously believed Lindsey in the early 1980s, I might have never gone to college and seminary. Why bother getting an education if Christ was returning in less than a decade? David and Michele's friend, along with many other people, faces a similar but more severe problem brought on by suggestive predictions.

Some respected evangelicals suggest dates without dogmatically affirming a particular date for the end. Some of these imply date predictions by quoting someone else who is setting a date. Or after listing a barrage of reasons why they personally believe 1988, 1999 or 2000 is the date of the end, they may issue a caveat: "This is all very interesting, but no one knows for sure when the end will take place."

Psalm 94 *might* secretly predict events in 1994, according to J. R. Church;[21] the Second Coming *might* occur in A.D. 2000, according to Grant Jeffrey.[22] Salem Kirban predicted that the United States would join the European nations under one dictator by 1990, adding the qualification that these things "may or may not come true."[23]

We should reject date-suggesting for at least three reasons.

First, date-suggesting encourages others to set dates and lends credibility to their arguments. The Hyoo-go or Rapture movement in Korea, for instance, reprinted on its tracts a suggestion by Jack Van Impe that 1992 could be the year of the rapture. D. A. Miller adopted a 1992 calculation made by Chuck Missler, a pastor on Christian radio who foreworded Miller's book *Forbidden Knowledge: Or Is It?* to support her September 1992 rapture.[24]

Second, date-suggesting flirts with being disobedient to Scripture. No one knows the time of the end, but we can certainly play a lot of guessing games. Imagine that a book has been published suggesting that we should speculate about the kind of woman or man we would want to marry if our current spouse were to pass away or desert us. Responsible Christian bookstore owners would promptly ban such a book, because it could easily become an incentive for committing adultery. Why then do many Christian teachers, knowing that date-setting is unbiblical, flirt with the practice?

Third, many people do not make a distinction between date-suggesting and date-setting. Unfortunately, these people sometimes respond by doing things that they regret later, after the prediction doesn't come to pass. What will happen to the woman who sold her assets to live in the country based on date-suggestions? What happens to people who forsake an education or trade, occupation, marriage, starting a family or buying a house because they believe the end is too near? Date-suggesting could easily cast a stumbling block before weak or younger Christians. We should seriously consider Paul's words: "It is better not to eat meat or drink wine or *to do anything else that will cause your brother to fall"* (Rom 14:21).

No one can discern the date, because Christ clearly taught that no one could know the time of his return (Mt 24:36; Acts 1:7).

3
Reasons Why
No One
<u>Can Get Around</u>
<u>Matthew 24:36</u>
<u>and Related Passages</u>

*T*he exact time had been revealed. The rapture was to happen at 24:00 hours on October 28, 1992. According to the Hyoo-go (Korean for "rapture") movement, on this day the rapture would occur at 6:00 p.m. Jewish time, six hours "behind" Korean time.[1] Extreme as this prediction appears, many end-time soothsayers continue predicting the date of the rapture or the Second Coming of Christ. How do they justify date-setting when biblical passages teach that no one knows the time of Christ's return? Regarding the time of his return, Jesus said in Matthew 24:35-36: "Heaven and earth will pass away, but my words will never pass away. No one knows about that day or hour, not even the angels in heaven, nor the Son, but only the Father" (compare Mk 13:32).

It seems odd for certain Christian teachers to claim they know the date for the world's end when Christ himself did not know it! This chapter will answer the arguments posed by date-setters who twist Matthew 24:36 and related passages into theological pretzels.

Reason 10: New Revelations Will Never Contradict Biblical Revelation

The Lord first called Bang Ik Ha—a twelve-year-old boy from Korea—in July 1987 at a midnight evangelical worship service. God allegedly told him, "Therefore, just as I have prepared John before the Son of Man came to the earth, again I am preparing Ha Bang Ik!"[2] God reportedly called Ha to prepare the way for the Second Coming of Christ: "God showed his mother Hyun Jung Lee in her dream a child with a sword and a book in his hand who was taller than mountains in the midst of storms and peals of thunder and blood. Then a scroll came down from Heaven that said 'the Book of Revelation.' " Ha would supposedly fulfill the prophecies in the book of Revelation.[3]

According to the Taberah World Mission, headed by this young prophet, true Christians can know the time of Christ's return. God allegedly commanded Bang Ik Ha's followers, "Know the time of My return! The ones who know the time of My return are blessed."[4] Those who denied that Christ would return in October 1992 were labeled heretics. God had reportedly said that those who did not discern the Second Coming's date would be punished.[5]

Based on Acts 1:7, Harold Camping affirms that the apostles did not know the time or season of Christ's coming. Christ wanted his disciples to focus on evangelism, not to spend their time trying to figure out the date of his return. That is why God hid the details of the end from believers for almost two thousand years. But now he has opened the "spiritual eyes" of some Christians so that the "mystery" of the end can be revealed. Camping understands Daniel 12:9-10 to mean that the date will be *unsealed* during the last days in which we now live, but only the wise will understand. Camping assures us that the Bible says "very clearly . . . there will be a revelation of additional truth at the end."[6]

Does the Bible permit further revelation? Since Scripture clearly teaches that no one knows the time of Christ's return, new revelations from God cannot contradict this. Jesus' warnings cannot be nullified: no one knows the time of his return, and no one can change these very words of Jesus until "heaven and earth will pass away" (Mt 24:35-36). According to Bible scholar R. C. H. Lenski, Christ claimed that no one will *ever* know the time of his return and the complete restoration of God's kingdom (Acts 1:7; compare Mt 19:28; Mk 10:35-39; Lk 22:24-30). The Father has "fixed" *(etheto)* these times, and they are beyond our reach.[7]

Camping resorts to circular reasoning when interpreting Daniel 12:9; in other words, he presupposes the very thing he tries to prove. Camping must already assume that we are living in the very last years of history to affirm that the seal of Daniel's prophecy—which is not to be opened until the end—can now be opened.

Daniel 12:9 does not state that Daniel sealed up some hidden meaning about the end which could only be revealed by end-time believers. As one commentary on Daniel notes, "The shutting up and sealing which was commanded to the prophet [Daniel] can therefore only consist in this, that the book should be preserved in security against any defacement of its contents, so that it might be capable of being read at all times down to the time of the end."[8]

Even if we assume that after Daniel's prophecies some further revelation might come, such revelation could only be New Testament prophecy. The prophetic seal of Daniel was opened by Jesus in Revelation 5:1-7 and will never be sealed again according to Revelation 22:10: "Do not seal up the words of the prophecy of this book, because the time is near." The seal of Daniel was in fact opened in the last days. As discussed in chapter two, "last days" stands for the entire New Testament church era (1 Cor 10:11; Heb 1:1-2; 1 Jn 2:18; Rev 1:3; 22:10). No new revelation about end-time events can now be added to these prophecies, and no new spiritual understanding can nullify them.

Reason 11: We Cannot Know the Day, Hour, Season or Time of the End

When I asked Larry, a representative of the Taberah World Mission, about Matthew 24:36, he replied in a quick, mechanical way. Bang Ik Ha has never claimed to know the *exact* day and hour of the rapture— only the month. Contrary to other groups in the Hyoo-go movement, Larry informed me that his prophet-leader did not necessarily believe the rapture would take place on October 28; but it would definitely take place *sometime* in October 1992.

Like Larry, many date-setters try to argue that even though Christ said no one knows the "day or hour" of his return, he did not say we cannot know the week, month or year. Based on this argument from silence, we can narrow down the time of the Second Coming or the rapture to the very week or month! For instance, prophecy writer Ron Reese admitted that he did not know the day or hour of prophetic events, but he nevertheless stated that the Great Tribulation would begin in 1992 or 1993, with the world ending about the year 2000.[9]

Edgar Whisenant writes: "If Jesus arrives at one particular instant of time, there are 24 zones around the world, and each time zone has multitudes of Christians in it. How are you going to identify that particular instant in each time zone on earth? . . . So you can see the problem in trying to tell all the Christians covering the earth at any one instant of time the exact day or hour of our Lord's return."[10] Is this how Jesus originally intended his followers to comprehend Matthew 24:36? Jesus did not have twenty-four time zones in mind. No such system existed at that time. Remember, America and the entire Western hemisphere were virtually unknown to people of Europe and the Mediterranean until the time of Columbus.

More important, the context of Matthew 24 does not support any date-setting whatsoever. After all, what would be the purpose of Christ's claim in Matthew 24:36 if we could still figure out the week or month of his return? And what would be the point behind the parable of the wicked servant in Matthew 24:42-51 if the servant could figure out the general time of his master's return? If we interposed Whisenant's date into the parable, couldn't the servant continue beating his fellow servants and getting drunk all the way until September 1988 without having to worry about his master dropping in unexpectedly? Couldn't the church of Sardis, not knowing the "time" of Christ's judgment (Rev 3:3), still know the day or week of that judgment and so continue in its spiritual sleep until then? Clearly, Matthew 24:36 does *not* imply that we can know the week, month or year of Christ's return though we can't know the hour or day (see Acts 1:7).

According to some date-setters' reasoning, Mark 13:35 could similarly be read to say that we *can* know the night of Jesus' return—just not in which quarter of the night he will come. But actually Jesus here lists the various watches of the night (each being normally three hours long) to stress the unknowability of his coming. Since we do not know the time of his return, we must keep spiritually awake (prepared) even during times ("night watches") when we may have a tendency to fall sleep (Rom 13:11-14; 1 Thess 5:1-11; Rev 3:1-6). We must "be on guard! Be alert! [We] do not know when that *time* will come" (Mk 13:33).

In Mark 13:33 the Greek word for time *(kairos)* refers to God's general appointed time, not a literal "day" or "hour." The word sometimes describes an entire era comprising many years (Rom 8:18; 2 Cor 6:2; 2 Tim 4:3; 1 Pet 1:10-11). And even the words *day (hēmera)* and *hour (hōra)* in certain contexts (such as Mt 24:36) refer to an extended period of time much longer than a literal day or hour. *Day* can mean a period lasting from several months to an indefinite number of years (Acts 8:1; Rom 13:12; 2 Cor 6:2; Phil 1:6; 2 Pet 3:8). The "Day of the Lord" lasts much longer than a mere twenty-four hours (2 Cor 1:14; 1 Thess 5:2; 2 Pet 3:10; Rev 16:14). Similarly, in certain contexts *hour* extends beyond a mere sixty minutes (Mt 26:45; Lk 22:53; Jn 2:4; 4:25; 7:30; 12:23, 27; 13:1; 17:1; Rev 3:3; 18:10, compare 18:8). Regarding the time of Christ's return, the limit of our ignorance extends far beyond a literal day or hour.

Reason 12: No One Can Get Around Acts 1:7

Only a few weeks after his resurrection, the disciples asked Jesus if he would now "restore the kingdom to Israel" (Acts 1:6). Jesus quickly responded, "It is not for you to know the times or dates the Father has set by his own authority" (1:7).

We do not know the "times or dates" that the Lord has appointed. Since "restoring the kingdom," for the disciples, would mean the end times, this passage speaks against all end-time date-setting (compare Mt 19:28; Mk 10:35-39; Lk 22:24-30).

Paul uses the same phrase, "times and dates," to exhort all Christians about the unexpectedness of Christ's coming (1 Thess 5:1-2). The Father has appointed these times and dates so that they are forever unknowable. No one will ever figure them out until they actually take place. No date predictions can fulfill God's timetable (2 Thess 2:7; 1 Tim 6:14-15; Tit 1:3).

The great Bible expositor F. F. Bruce interpreted "it is not for you" in Acts 1:7 as "it does not belong to you" (Greek: *ouch hymōn estin;* literally, "it is not of you") to know the times and seasons. This nuance reflects the idea that Christ was telling the disciples, "It is not your concern to know the times and dates."[11] In popular English this would mean "It is none of your business to know the dates of future events which my Father has appointed."

Remember, this was not a new teaching. Christ had already taught that the kingdom of God could not be observed through signs (Lk 17:20; compare Lk 21:8).

With such strong warnings against date-setting, it's amazing how date-setters presumptuously reinterpret Acts 1:7. In order to get around this verse some authors twist the Greek. Edgar Whisenant argued that the phrase "the times or seasons" in Greek meant a very specific point, referring back to the terms *day* and *hour* in Matthew

24:36.[12] Christians were told that they could not know the day or hour of the September 1988 rapture, but, standing Acts 1:7 on its head, Whisenant claimed they *could* know the time and season!

Contrary to Whisenant, the Greek words in Acts 1:7 for "times" and "dates" *(chronos* and *kairos)* cannot be reduced to the Greek words for "day" and "hour" *(hēmera* and *hōra).* Both words refer to time periods that could last many years. In Acts 1:21 the word *time (chronos),* which is commonly defined as a duration or span of time and means "year" in modern Greek, refers to the entire three-and-a-half-year ministry of Jesus. It can also refer to a generation of forty years (Acts 13:18), or even an entire lifetime or longer (Acts 17:30; 1 Cor 7:39; 1 Pet 4:3).

The word *dates* ("seasons" in the King James Version), which is *kairos* in Greek, is commonly understood as a decisive point, "often with a stress on the fact that it is divinely ordained"[13]; it can refer to a year (Rev 12:12-14; compare 12:6), a season or a few years (Lk 4:13; Acts 14:17; Gal 4:10; 6:9; Philem 15), a former disposition or an entire lifetime (Mk 10:30; Rom 2:12; 8:18), or the entire New Testament era (Lk 21:24; Rom 3:25-26; 2 Cor 6:2; 1 Pet 1:10-11). In the Greek version of the Old Testament (called the Septuagint or LXX) *kairos* and *chronos* are connected together and refer to entire eras of successive kingdoms (Dan 2:21; compare 2:31-44). In Acts 1:7 Jesus clearly intended *times* and *dates* to mean much more than just a few weeks or months. He is saying we cannot figure out the date of the end—period. Another way of rendering the combination of *times* and *dates* is this: "It is not for you to know the various epochs of history *[kairoi],* nor yet how long they will last *[chronoi];* for these are matters of God's own knowledge and disposal."[14]

Reason 13: The Original Greek Language Does Not Support Date-Setting

Mission for the Coming Days, the leading church of the Hyoo-go movement, made a distinction between two Greek words for "know" in their interpretation of Matthew 24:36: *oida* and *ginōskō*. Church leaders suggested the word *oida* means "to know without effort" or "to know right away." This is the word for "know" used in Matthew 24:36 and Mark 13:32. According to their reasoning, then, Jesus was saying Christians cannot know the day or hour automatically (that is, intuitively or without effort), but that they must make an effort to study in order to know the day and hour. In other words, believers *can* know the exact day and hour after doing a little bit of homework! According to Mission for the Coming Days literature, if these passages had used *ginōskō* ("perceive," "recognize," "understand") instead of *oida,* Jesus would have been saying that even after studying there would be no way to know the day or hour of his return.[15]

Is there a significant distinction between Greek meanings of the verb translated "know"? Hardly. Jesus uses *ginōskō* and *oida* interchangeably (compare Mt 24:39, 43, 50 *[ginōskō]* with Mt 24:36, 42 *[oida]*). In fact, in Acts 1:7, when telling the disciples that no one knows the time when he will completely restore the kingdom of God, Jesus uses *ginōskō* for "know" instead of *oida*. Remember, according to Mission for the Coming Days, the use of *ginōskō* in this context must mean that even after intense study we cannot know the time of the Lord's return! Furthermore, in certain contexts *oida* refers to a knowledge that requires much thought and effort (Mk 4:13; Eph 1:18). Since these two verbs are used interchangeably in Matthew 24 and elsewhere, there is no basis for making a technical distinction between them.[16]

Reason 14: "No One Knows" the Time of the End Does Not Mean "No One Has Yet Experienced" the Time of the End

Harold Camping suggests that the phrase "no one knows" in Mark 13:32 really means that no one has yet experienced Judgment Day. In Camping's view, Jesus did not know the time of his own return only in the sense that he had not yet experienced the coming judgment. He did know the date, however, and so can we.[17]

But if Jesus wanted his disciples to reinterpret *knows* as "experiences" in Mark 13:32, why didn't he simply say so? He could have used other Greek words that can mean "experience," such as *geuomai* (Heb 2:9; 6:4-5 C. B. Williams; TEV), or perhaps used an auxiliary verb with the noun *peira* (compare Heb 11:36 NASB), or *pathēma* (as in 1 Pet 5:9 NASB).[18] Camping cannot cite any legitimate version of the Bible that translates *knows (oida)* as "experiences" in Mark 13:32. In fact, if we substituted "experiences" for *knows* in Mark 13:32-37, the context would not make sense.

Reason 15: Setting Matthew 24:36 in a Different Period from the Great Tribulation Does Not Allow Us to Know the Date

End-time date-setter Martin Hunter teaches that Matthew 24:36 describes the time at the *end* of the millennium (the thousand-year reign of Christ), not the time of Christ's Second Coming, which he believes will happen before the millennium. He cites Matthew 24:35: "Heaven and earth will pass away." This supposedly refers to the destruction of the earth after the thousand-year reign of Christ (Rev 20—21). Although we cannot know the date of the end of the millennium, we *can* know the date of Christ's Second Coming, which he claims will take place December 25, 1999.[19]

On a similar note, D. A. Miller claims we can know the date of the rapture but not the date of the Second Coming. Matthew 24:36 only refers to the latter.[20] Miller's position presupposes that the rapture will begin before the Great Tribulation, while the Second Coming occurs after it. Many Christians are not willing to grant her this premise.[21] Nevertheless, let us assume the rapture will take place before the Great Tribulation. Her teaching still fails because 1 Thessalonians 4:13—5:11 ties in the rapture with "times and dates" and the Lord's return as a "thief in the night" (compare Acts 1:7). As explained in reason 2, Paul is reaffirming to the Thessalonians something they already knew: no one can know the date of the Day of the Lord, which includes the date of the rapture. When Christ said no one knows the time of his return, he included present-day believers (Mk 13:37; Lk 12:41-48).

Hunter's interpretation of Matthew 24:36 is out of context. The passage clearly refers to the Lord's return and does not even mention the millennium (see Mt 24:3, 30-31, 37, 42-44). When Jesus says, "Heaven and earth will pass away," he is not referring to the millennium. Rather, he is comparing the temporal character of this present age—which passes away—with the permanence of his prophetic words, which "will never pass away."

But let's suppose that Hunter was right—Jesus *was* referring to the millennium. Given Hunter's literal interpretation of the millennium, if Jesus is saying that no one knows the time of the millennium's end, he lied—because all we have to do is add 1,000 to the date of Christ's return, December 25, 1999, and we have the exact date for the end of the millennium!

Reason 16: Even After His Ascension, Jesus Did Not Reveal the Date

False prophecy inevitably breeds heresy, and groups that set end-time dates unfortunately follow this principle. Prior to October 28, 1992, Mission for the Coming Days taught that Jesus did not know the date of his return because he gave up his deity during his life on earth (Mk 13:32). This was why he called himself the Son of Man. But now that he is in heaven, he has regained his former knowledge as God and is revealing the date to his followers.[22] In effect, Mission for the Coming Days denied that Jesus was fully God when he was manifested in the flesh.

The Bible, however, continues to portray Jesus as the Son of Man even after he returns to glory (Mt 24:30; compare Heb 13:8). In fact, the term "Son of Man" can actually refer to Christ's deity, not merely his humanity (Dan 7:9-14; Jn 3:13; 5:27; 6:62; Acts 7:55-60). Additionally, Jesus did not lose his deity during his incarnation (Jn 8:23-58; 16:29-30; 20:28; 21:17; Phil 2:5-11; Heb 13:8). He voluntarily declined to use his omniscience (all-knowing ability) to discover the date of his return.[23] He did not know the date of his return because it was not God the Father's will for him to know it.

In fact, God does not want *anyone* to know the date of Christ's return. Those who attempt to figure out the date sin by setting themselves against God's will.

Reason 17: Spiritual Fervor Is Not a Good Enough Reason to Set Dates

In her book *Watch and Be Ready! 1992 Millions Disappear* D. A. Miller claims, "God is a date setter." Ignorance of the date of the Lord's return causes a lack of fervor, she says, like that of a couple who claim to be madly in love but refuse to set a date for their wedding. She adds: "Stockbrokers, doctors, weathermen and military agents are rewarded for their attempts to determine the future, but the religious community pounces upon those who try to understand and apply the prophetic portions of the Bible."[24]

The reason the "religious community pounces" on date-setters is obvious: they are disobeying the Lord's words in Matthew 24:36 and related passages. No doubt, people who think they know the date of the end are often zealous. But should we disobey the Word of God for the sake of zeal? The end does not justify the means. God is not impressed by our fervor if it entails disobedience (see 1 Sam 15:22-23; Mt 7:21-23).

When Christians deny what Scripture clearly teaches, they set themselves up for either self-deception or demonic deception (Jer 23:16; 1 Tim 4:1-4). The Bible teaches us the exact opposite of what doomsday advocates teach. We do not know the time of the Lord's return. Date-setting ventures into areas that God has expressly declared off-limits; hence it is an act of disobedience. Setting dates for the end, whether through visions or by reading between the lines of Scripture, is not much different from practicing the forbidden arts of astrology and fortunetelling.

4
Reasons Why No One Can Decode a Secret Date for the Second Coming

L et's do some number calculations. The year of the Declaration of Independence is A.D. 1776. If we add the first and last number of 1776 (1 + 6 = 7), this will give us a third 7, making 777. Now if we subtract 777 from 1776, we'll get 999.

About a century ago, a Christian numerologist named Ivan Panin defended the Bible's authority by pointing out the numerous multiples of 7 hidden beneath the texts. Calculating Genesis 1:1, for instance, Panin discovered this verse had seven words and twenty-eight letters, or 4 × 7. Are such calculations significant?

Bible-numerics buster Oswald Allis noted that the first seven words of the Constitution, "We the people of the United States," also contain twenty-eight letters. So do such everyday sentences as "We had tea and toast for breakfast," "Hurry, girls, or we'll miss the train," "Their silly talk bored me to death" and so on.[1] Though well intentioned, Panin's calculations tell us nothing.

Numerology becomes dangerous in the hands of teachers who believe that every number in the Bible unveils a hidden meaning. In the Middle Ages, Christian mystics commonly interpreted the number 2 as the diversity between heaven and earth, 5 as the number of the flesh, 6 as the number of earthly perfection and so forth. During the same period, Jewish mystics followed the teachings of the Cabala, an occultic work laden with numerology. Today numerology is alive and well and continues to thrive in our churches.

Manipulating the numbers of Scripture is a common activity among date-setters. For example, end-times author Salty Dok subtracts 1,290 days from 1,335 days in Daniel 12:11-12, the answer being 45. These 45 days are then converted into years and added to 1948—the year Israel became a nation—to yield 1993. Dok then adds three and a half years to this date, based on Daniel 9:27, and winds up with November 1996 for the return of Christ.[2]

Such mathematical methods render the Bible meaningless. With enough numbers, a date-setter can interpret Scripture virtually any way he or she wishes. But let's examine some more end-time dates based on numerology.

Reason 18: No Numbers in the Bible Calculate to the Date of the End

Harold Camping frequently manipulated biblical numbers to arrive at his 1994 date. The two thousand cubits separating the priests from the Hebrews in Joshua 3:3-4 signified two thousand years from the birth of Christ (7 B.C.) to 1994, and the two thousand demon-possessed swine that drowned in Mark 5 also affirmed this date![3] The first world lasted 6,023 years before God destroyed it by the flood in Noah's time, which—contrary to virtually everyone—Camping claimed took place in 4990 B.C. Adding 7,000 years to 4990 B.C., he arrived at A.D. 2011. Once at this date, he arbitrarily subtracted 23 years (which, he claimed, represents the final tribulation) because the days of tribulation "will be shortened" (Mt 24:22), and thus arrived at May 21, 1988.[4] Invariably, every path leads to his ultimate date for Christ's return—after September 6, 1994. Camping taught that the final tribulation will last 2,300 days (six years and four months) according to Daniel 8:14, beginning in 1988 and continuing until Christ's return in 1994.[5]

It gets worse. Camping once believed that "the entire New Testament era, from the time of the cross to Judgment Day, is typified by 1260 days or 3½ years."[6] But later—defying reason—he announced that the "forty-two months" mentioned in Revelation 13:5 actually means three and a half days, which in turn was converted to 84 hours (or 2 × 42), and 8,401 days (which he rounded off to 8,400). He then recycled these days to 23 years, based on modern calculations of 365.2422 days per year. This supposedly coincides with Daniel's 2,300 days, amounting to approximately six years and four months for the final tribulation.[7]

Let us untangle Camping's confusing web of dates and numbers. Comparing Revelation 13:5 with Revelation 12:14, note that this prophecy mentions three and a half *times* (*kairos* in Greek), not *days* (*hēmera* in Greek). The three and a half times are equivalent to 42 months (Rev 11:2; 12:14; 13:5) and 1,260 days (Rev 11:3; 12:6). In fact, after the two witnesses of Revelation 11 minister for three and a half *years,* they will be killed and remain unburied for three and a half *days* (Rev 11:9). Revelation 11—13 clearly distinguishes between days and years, so Camping was flat-out wrong. Moreover, where in the Bible are we given license to convert three and a half days into 84 hours, or to calculate biblical figures by our modern notion of 365.2422 days when first-century Jews followed a lunisolar calendar averaging 364 days per year? There is no biblical warrant for such calculations.

Finally, what external evidence did Camping cite to affirm the significance of May 1988 as the onslaught for the final tribulation *that was not the case before that time, but has been the case ever since?* There is simply no evidence that apostate activities, which he held to be the end-time sign, significantly accelerated beginning May 21, 1988. There is also no evidence that a number of entire denominations that were not apostate prior to May 1988 have now become apostate.

In fact, statistics show evidence to the contrary. American baby boomers are returning to the churches they once abandoned in the 1960s and 1970s. According to the Barna Report, 43 percent of Americans attended church in 1988, the beginning of the alleged apostasy. Instead of undergoing a significant drop in 1989, church attendance actually increased by 2 percent. In 1991 total church attendance went up to 49 percent, and the number of people calling the Bible "important" for their daily living soared 12 percent higher from 1991 to 1992. These statistics, though not definitive, generally indicate church growth instead of a massive falling away from the church. And Barna's studies do not even address the major Christian revivals occurring in countries beyond the United States. Thus the widespread apostasy that Camping envisions corresponds neither to Scripture nor to current reality.[8]

Reason 19: Numbers in the Bible Do Not Have a Hidden Meaning That Gives Us the Date of the End

Date-setters often employ another numerology tactic called term-switching. Numbers are baptized with spiritual meanings whenever those meanings support the date-setter's theory. Harold Camping converted the number 17 into the number that represents heaven. Then he reminded the reader how the seventeen-year-old Joseph—a type of Christ— had a dream about ruling over his family (Gen 37:5-7). Also, Joseph's father, Jacob, stayed under Joseph's care in Egypt for seventeen years, and this, Camping claimed, depicts our spending eternity with Christ. He then multiplied 2 × 17 (34) and multiplied that product by 100 to get 3,400. When this number was added to 1407 B.C. (the entrance of Israel into the land of Canaan), it brought Camping to 1994.[9]

If the number 17 represents heaven in the Bible, we should expect it to do so consistently; otherwise it would lose its significance. But when we examine the Scriptures, we find that no such meaning can be poured into other passages that contain the number 17 (such as 1 Chron 7:11). Actually, we could arbitrarily make 17 mean almost anything. Suppose 17 secretly means "wickedness." Could we justify this? Absolutely. After all, the wicked reigns of both Rehoboam and Joash lasted seventeen years (2 Chron 12:13-14; 2 Kings 13:1-2). When we add the seven heads and ten horns of the dragon in Revelation 12, we also get 17!

There are dozens of meanings we could assign to this number, or for that matter any other number. What makes Camping's interpretation better than that of anyone else? And why should the number 17 necessarily represent heaven in the passages Camping cites? Since Joseph was seventeen when he had his dream, we could interpret 17 as the number of visions and dreams—or, in Jacob's case, the number of old age.

When a date-setter plays with biblical numbers, the plain meaning of Scripture is often abandoned in favor of a hidden meaning. This form of Scripture-twisting, used by a number of doomsday evangelicals, is also practiced by cult leaders. Whenever the literal interpretation of a verse contradicts their false doctrine, they reinterpret the passage, giving it a "spiritual" or "hidden" meaning. How can we justify such a method of interpretation in the church while we condemn cultists for using it?

Since Camping believes that hidden meanings underlie all Scripture—including biblical numbers—he, like the Jehovah's Witnesses and Mormons, can create such meanings to support virtually any date or doctrine he wishes. Once the hidden message no longer suits his taste, he can simply change it. He violates accepted principles of interpretation (called hermeneutics) by interpreting the Scriptures subjectively (that is, interpreting the Bible according to what he wants it to say) instead of objectively (trying to discern and obey what the Bible actually says).

The Bible is not a watermelon. We cannot eat only what we like and spit out what we don't like. If I claim to be a Christian but am an adulterer, I cannot erase or reinterpret the Scriptures that condemn adultery just because they contradict my behavior. I must either turn away from my adultery or quit calling myself a Christian. In the same way, Christians must not discard or reinterpret passages that plainly declare we cannot know the time of the Lord's return (Mt 24:36; Acts 1:7). We are called to surrender our conduct, our doctrine, our ambitions and our very lives to the plain teachings of Scripture. The Word of God does not submit to us—we submit to it.

As a general rule, we should look first for Scripture's plain meaning. We need to consider possible figurative meanings if the text does not "make sense" on a literal level (for example, Is 55:12, "the trees of the field will clap their hands") or if the context supports a figurative meaning (for example, John 10:7, "I am the gate"). Certain portions of prophetic books such as Revelation, often called "apocalyptic literature," need to be interpreted symbolically (such as Rev 5:6: "Then I saw a Lamb. . . . He had seven horns and seven eyes, which are the seven spirits of God sent out into all the earth"). Yet even apocalyptic writings give us no basis for calculating numbers into new hidden variables. We are not given biblical warrant to interpret 666 as 3 × 222 and then spiritualize the meaning of the numbers 3 and 2. Scripture should be read for what it clearly, figuratively or symbolically says—not for some coded message hidden between the lines. If anyone (especially one who is not a scholar[10]) claims to have found a hidden meaning in Scripture that nobody else or very few other people seem to have discovered, watch out!

Even the number 7, which has some symbolic significance in Scripture (sometimes conveying an idea of completeness, as in Mt 18:21-22), should never be given a *hidden* significance. In Genesis 41, when Joseph interpreted seven lean cows in a dream as seven years of famine, he did not multiply the seven lean cows with the seven fat cows to get forty-nine years! Seven remains seven, and 666 remains 666.

And the Bible nowhere implies that the number 17 means anything other than seventeen! We must always respect the original intent of the authors of Scripture.

When reading the Bible, ask yourself: "How did the author intend his readers to understand this passage?" Undoubtedly the authors of Scripture were not working with the convoluted logic of today's date-setters. The chart below demonstrates how numbers can mean practically anything.[11]

Number	E. W. Bullinger	Cornelius Agrippa	Harold Camping
1	unity	purpose	———
2	difference	balance	church
3	completeness	versatility	God's purpose
4	works	steadiness	universal
5	grace	adventure	grace/judgment
6	human number	dependable	———
7	perfection	mystery	perfection
8	resurrection	success	———
9	finality	achievement	———
10	ordinal perfection	———	completion
12	government perfection	———	fullness
17	spirit/order	———	heaven

Reason 20: The End-Time Date Itself Carries No Hidden Meaning

What is significant about 1991? Rick Henry Hall, founder of Spirit of Prophecy Ministries in Las Vegas, claimed:

> The Year, 1991, is the only year in this final Chapter of the days of labor that reads the same, frontwards and backwards. 1991 or 1991! Either way you might read it, with knowledge of the Biblical numbers, = UNITY WITH GOD and ONENESS WITH THE CREATOR! When we add them together we have $1 + 9 + 9 + 1 = 20$ or $2 + 0 = 2$ and two (2) is the biblical number of a *DIVISION!* This is the year that God will DIVIDE His covenanted by heart and spirit People and meet them in the clouds of glory.[12]

In a similar manner, Harold Camping claims that 1994 ($1 + 9 + 9 + 4$) equals 23—representing a 2,300-day final tribulation.[13]

Do the numbers in dates have any special significance? Not at all. We could play word and number games to make any date seem portentous. Consider the number 28. We could build an erroneous case that the end of the world will occur in 1999 because $1 + 9 + 9 + 9 = 28$, and 28 represents judgment because King Jehu, who judged the wicked house of Ahab, reigned twenty-eight years (2 Kings 10:36). Now let's do some mathematics:

Count the vowels in the name Harold Camping = 4.

Multiply this by the total letters in Camping: $4 \times 7 = 28 = 2 \times 2 \times 7$.

Now change the multiplication signs to addition: $2 + 2 + 7 = 11$.

Subtract 11 from 28 = 17 (one of Camping's significant prophetic numbers).

Now add 17 to the number of letters in Harold: $17 + 6 = 23$ (Camping's other significant prophetic number).

Harold = 6 letters. The numeric value of the consonants of his name is $[H (8) + R (18) + L (12) + D (4)] = 42 = 6 \times 7$.

Find the numeric value of the vowels in his first name: $[A (1) + O (15)] = 16$.

Multiply the value of the consonants times the value of the vowels: 42 × 16 = 672 = **6** × 112.

Note: there are a total of three sixes, or **666.**

Find the total numerical value of his first name: 42 + 16 = 58.

Multiply this by the total numeric value of his last name, Camping: 58 × 63 = 3654.

Split 3654 into 36 and 54: (**6** × **6**) and (**6** × 9). Once again, there are three sixes, or **666.**

Of course these games are nothing more than clever inventions. So why should anyone believe the games played by date-setters? My play on Camping's name shows how subjectively any number can be manipulated to justify any date one wishes to prove.

Reason 21: Chapter and Verse Numbers Do Not Give Us the Date of the End

Edgar Whisenant claimed that Psalms 88 to 94 corresponded to the Great Tribulation period that would occur from 1988 to 1994. (He based this speculation on the teachings of Joe Civelli and J. R. Church.) He stressed that these psalms constitute the direst songs in all the Bible.[14] J. R. Church, whose book *Hidden Prophecies in the Psalms* sold over 100,000 copies, implies that Psalms 90—100 probe into the events of the final decade before the messianic era and that 1997 might be the date of the rapture.[15] What is significant about these chapters? Church points out that the phrase "all generations" appears in Psalms 90 and 100 and that these chapters appear within the boundaries of the "last generation" mentioned in Psalms 48 and 102—a hint that the final generation extends from A.D. 1948 to 2002.

Church fails to mention, however, that the phrase "all generations" appears over a dozen times in Psalms, the first in 33:11 and the last in 146:10. What's more, the reference to "last generation" is misleading. The psalms actually mention not a "last generation" but a generation that is to come, a "future generation" (as in Ps 102:18). The context is a reminder that the teachings of the psalms should be passed down from generation to generation. From the psalmist David's perspective, this would mean passing his songs to his son Solomon, and then Solomon passing them down to his son and so on. The "future generation" phrase appears in other psalms such as 22, 78 and 109 and bears no significance regarding doomsday dates.

Besides, who made the chapters of Psalms a prophetic calendar for end-time events? If we assume 2046 is the date of Christ's coming based on the "all generations" in Psalm 146, what happens if that year passes with no Messiah? Perhaps then we'll need to seek out all occurrences of the word *generation* in the book of Proverbs!

Chapter numbers can never give us a prophetic time frame, because these numbers are not inspired Scripture. Our present-day chapter divisions were included in the Bible in the twelfth century under the auspices of Archbishop of Canterbury Stephen Langton and in the thirteenth century at the initiative of Cardinal Hugo. And verse divisions did not come about until the sixteenth century, under Robert Etienne (Stephanus). Before that time the reader could not turn to a chapter and verse, such as John 3:16. He or she simply had to peruse the Gospel of John to find the words "For God so loved the world." Given the date-setters' abuse of chapter numbers, maybe the chapter and verse divisions should never have been made.[16]

Reason 22: The Feast of Tabernacles Does Not Give Us the Date of the End

Have you ever wondered why a large percentage of end-time dates seem to fall in September and October? Nearly always it is because the date-setter has used the date of the Jewish Feast of Tabernacles—a feast that needs to be fulfilled, according to many prophecy teachers. The Jewish feasts are described in Leviticus 23—25 and Numbers 29. The Jews celebrated the Feast of Tabernacles in Tishri, the first month of their calendar. Included in this month are Rosh Hashanah (head of the year) and Yom Kippur (the Day of Atonement).

Prophecy buffs reason that the Passover feast found its fulfillment during Christ's crucifixion, resurrection and ascension, and Pentecost was fulfilled in Acts 2, but the Feast of Tabernacles still awaits fulfillment. This will happen during the final moments of the end times. Doomsday teacher Charles R. Taylor writes, "*Rosh Hashana of Sept. 6, 1994 will start the last 7-year cycle of this century* and most likely will usher in the prophesied seven year Tribulation Period so that the Rosh Hashana (Jewish New Year) of the year 2001 can begin the millennium—the 1,000 year era of the marvelous reign of the Messiah."[17]

There is just one crucial problem: the Feast of Tabernacles pertained only to the nation of Israel under the Law of Moses. As New Testament believers, we are no longer bound by the Law of Moses, nor are we required to literally observe any of the feasts kept by the Israelites (though many Messianic Jews do so in appreciation of their heritage). All such requirements were fulfilled in Christ (Rom 10:4; 13:8-10; Gal 2—3; Heb 7:12-25; 8:1—10:18; 10:5-10). Colossians 2:16-17 states: "Therefore do not let anyone judge you by what you eat or drink, or with regard to a religious festival, a New Moon celebration or a Sabbath day. These are a shadow of the things that were to come; the reality, however, is found in Christ." Unfortunately, date-setters want to embrace the shadow instead of the reality.

Reason 23: The Year of Jubilee Does Not Give Us the Date of the End

According to Leviticus 25:2-9, God commanded the Israelites to observe every seventh year as a sabbath, and after seven such sabbath years (forty-nine years) came the Year of Jubilee, in which Israelites were freed from all debts. Harold Camping claims the first Jubilee occurred fifty years after the Israelite entrance into Canaan (1407 B.C.), or 1357 B.C. Counting by fifties from that date, A.D. 1994 is Jubilee 68, or $2 \times 2 \times 17$ (spiritually speaking, "the universality of the church" times "heaven"). Camping also teaches that the first Jubilee calculated in Daniel's seventy weeks (Dan 9:24-27) was in 457 B.C., and

1994 is the fiftieth Jubilee since that time.[18]

The problem is that each doomsday-setter has his or her own Jubilee calendar. Even fifty-year cycles can be adjusted to fit into practically anyone's prophecy scheme as long as the right starting point is chosen. Edgar Whisenant inserts his starting point at Abraham's covenant with God in 1872 B.C. (minus 430 years of Hebrew captivity) to arrive at the seventieth Jubilee in 1988.[19] Joe Civelli starts his Jubilee from the Hebrew entrance into the land of Canaan, which he puts at 1436 B.C., so that 1995-1996 brings the seventieth Jubilee and the return of Christ.[20] Marvin Byers counts one Jubilee from 1947 to 1996.[21] Grant Jeffrey has three starting points for his Jubilee: the time of Adam, Joshua's Canaan entrance and Jesus' message in Luke 4:18-21.[22] He arbitrarily calculates these starting points into a mathematical formula based on a combination of the so-called 360-day prophetic years and the modern year of 365.25 days—neither of which the Jews observed. And contrary to both Camping and Civelli, Jeffrey claims the year the Israelites entered Canaan was 1451 B.C.

Why is there no agreement on the starting point? This question leads to the death blow for Jubilee juggling.

First, the Israelites could not have celebrated Jubilee before the entrance into Canaan, since Jubilee required that the Israelites own land. No Jubilee was ever celebrated during the time of Adam or that of Abraham; Israel had not yet come into being as a nation.

Second, it is doubtful whether the Israelites would have observed the Year of Jubilee precisely fifty years after entering the land of Canaan in 1407 B.C. (if indeed this is the correct date). Even after they came into Canaan, it took about six more years (perhaps up to 1401 B.C.) to conquer the Canaanite strongholds (Josh 14:1-10; compare Num 14:1-34).

Third, given the quickly degenerating morality of the Israelites as described in the book of Judges, we can guess that they probably did not celebrate any Jubilees during that era. In fact, there is no biblical or historical evidence that the Year of Jubilee was ever celebrated in any era. This despite the fact that both the Bible and history record the celebration of other Jewish holidays such as the Passover (for example, Josephus *Antiquities* 17.9.3; 2 Chron 30:13; Ezra 6:22; Mt 26:17), Pentecost (Josephus *Wars* 2.3.1; Acts 2:1) and the Feast of Tabernacles (*Antiquities* 13.8.2; Ezra 3:4; Jn 7:2-33).

Fourth, even if the Year of Jubilee was celebrated, it would be impossible for the Jews to have celebrated it consistently. They were taken captive by the Babylonians about 587 B.C. and did not return to Jerusalem until at least 539 B.C. The land of Israel was to lie desolate for seventy years because the Israelites had failed to observe sabbath years over a span of 490 years (2 Chron 36:21). If they failed to keep any of their sabbath years, it is inconceivable that they would have kept their Jubilee years, which were also sabbath years. And ever since Rome sacked Jerusalem in A.D. 70, the Jews have not been able to celebrate Jubilee. On what basis do date-setters calculate Jewish Jubilee cycles without a Jewish land in which they could have been celebrated?

Even since Israel reestablished itself in 1948, it has not officially observed the Year of Jubilee. Finally, there is no evidence that the New Testament saints celebrated Jubilee. Like the other feasts, the Year of Jubilee found its fulfillment in Christ (Lk 4:18-21; Col 2:14-17).

Reason 24: Numerology Is Not a Valid Way to Interpret Scripture

Should Christians calculate numbers from the Bible to support their beliefs? Where in Scripture do we find anyone using such a method? Certain numbers may have *some* significance. Numbers such as 7, 12, 40 and 144,000 may convey symbolic meanings. As I noted above, in Genesis 41 Joseph interpreted the seven lean cows of Pharaoh's dream as seven years of famine. In Revelation 13 the number 666 stands for the mark of the Beast. Scriptures containing symbolic numbers usually fall under the classification called apocalyptic literature.[23] We can usually determine whether a number has a symbolic meaning by (1) determining if we are reading apocalyptic literature, (2) examining the context of the mention of a particular number, (3) comparing Scripture with Scripture and (4) checking our conclusions with those of a reputable scholar or commentary.[24]

Date-setters, on the other hand, sometimes focus on numbers not only from apocalyptic segments of Scripture but from *any* segment, whether the style is narrative, poetry or prose. From Acts 27 Harold Camping factors the 276 men in the ship to get 23 × 12 and then uses the number 23 to signify the final tribulation of the church.[25] The book of Acts is not apocalyptic literature; it is a narrative. Neither the Holy Spirit nor Luke (the writer of Acts) intended this book to be interpreted in a prophetic manner.

The origin of this type of numerology was not the Bible. It developed through Egyptian and Babylonian religious worship.[26] And such numerological interpretations were entirely subject to whatever the interpreter desired a number to mean.

But the principal reason to reject date-setting numerology is that it is unbiblical. I encourage any follower of numerology to look up (through an exhaustive concordance) the numbers used by doomsday teachers and see if the hidden meaning assigned by the numerologist fits every instance where that number appears in Scripture. Does the date-setter's meaning honestly fit every passage without taking it out of context or spiritualizing the passage away? If you cannot arrive at the conclusion date-setters suggest *without their help,* then you can be sure God never intended that passage to be interpreted as they have done.

Even when a number does fit the meaning a date-setter assigns to it, is his or her meaning the only possible alternative? Can you think of counterexamples, other possible meanings or other ways to understand the number?

After your investigation, you will realize that you or anyone else, using mathematics, could manipulate Scripture to arrive at any desired date. Why not settle for the objective, plain interpretation of Scripture instead of subjective mathematical convolutions? We do well to heed Paul's warnings: "Command certain men not to teach false doctrines any longer nor to devote themselves to myths and endless genealogies. These promote controversies rather than God's work—which is by faith" (1 Tim 1:3-4). We need to "avoid foolish controversies . . . because these are unprofitable and useless" (Tit 3:9).

Oswald T. Allis writes:

The attempt to find mysterious numerical patterns and values in sentences, words, and phrases which have a plain and obvious meaning, whether the meaning is sublime or trite or trivial, whether it is found in the Bible, or in a masterpiece of secular literature, or in the commonplaces of ordinary life, is to say the least a tremendous waste of time and effort; and what is far more important, resting as it does on principles that are demonstrably false, it may lead to serious and disastrous consequences.[27]

Reason 25: Bible Chronology Does Not Give Us the Date of the End

William Miller spent two years of his life fervently searching the Scriptures. He finally uncovered the year of the Lord's return—1843. Starting at the beginning of the seventy weeks in Daniel 9:24 (457 B.C.) and converting twenty-three hundred evenings and mornings (Dan 8:14) to twenty-three hundred years, he added 2,300 to 457 and presto: A.D. 1843! He later changed the date to 1844, but Christ failed to appear on either date. This event—big news back then—was known in American history as the Great Disappointment. Miller's followers, known as the Millerites, branched off into several Adventist groups, of which the most popular became the Seventh-day Adventists.

Some doomsday advocates set dates by adding an alleged significant number (such as 2,300) to a significant event in history (such as the rebuilding of Jerusalem in 457 B.C.), and then propose a date for Christ's return.

Based on his bizarre interpretation of the genealogies in Genesis 5 and 11, Harold Camping calculates the earth's creation at 11,013 B.C.

and then adds 1988 (his date for the beginning of the Final Tribulation) to 11,013 to arrive at 13,000. The number 13, according to Camping, signifies "super fullness," confirming the end of the world.[28] Reportedly, Jesus was born somewhere between October 1 and 4 in 7 B.C. He was allegedly baptized when he was about thirty-five years old in A.D. 29, and he died on the cross in A.D. 33. Camping relentlessly combines these dates (7 B.C. and A.D. 33) with an array of other supposedly significant numbers to support his 1994 prediction. Perhaps his most popular system is simply to add the number 2,000 to 7 B.C. to get 1994.[29]

Extremes of mathematic madness crop up even in the "reputable" evangelical fold. Grant Jeffrey resurrects an old argument by Charles Taze Russell and the Watchtower (the Jehovah's Witnesses) when he speculates that "the times of the Gentiles," allegedly beginning in 606 B.C., lasted 2,520 years and ended in A.D. 1914. Then he adds a new twist by saying that the earlier "students of prophecy" made only one mistake: they forgot to calculate their years by Jeffrey's "biblical" 360-day years. Recalculated, the times of the Gentiles ended in the autumn of A.D. 1878 (and don't bother looking for a significant historical event that would confirm that "the times of the Gentiles" ended then). However, according to Jeffrey, God gave the people 120 years to repent in the days of Noah (compare Gen 6). So Jeffrey then calculates that 120 "biblical" years amount to 118.3 calendar years; he adds this number to 1878 to make A.D. 1997 the official end of "the times of the Gentiles."[30]

It's remarkable that an evangelical would incorporate an argument promoted by a cultist like Charles Taze Russell. Interestingly, Russell himself was influenced by early Adventist teachings, whose roots lay in the Millerites and the 1844 Great Disappointment.

With all the date-setting of the 1990s, we are fast approaching another Great Disappointment: A.D. 2000. Instead of learning from history, Christian soothsayers seem doomed to repeat it.

5

Reasons Why No One Knows If the Millennium Will Start in A.D. 2000

F or the reasonable price of $19.99, the Millennium Society— spearheaded by Anchorage district attorney Edward E. McNally—will grant you entrance to a Woodstock-type festival, "the largest celebration in the history of the human race," come the year 2000.[1] In the music industry there's Prince with his apocalyptic CDs and song *1999*. On the silver screen there was Arnold Schwarzenegger starring in *Terminator 2: Judgment Day,* the biggest box-office hit of 1991 (topping the $200 million mark). You can find millennium journals, yearbooks and skin-care products, even a New York hotel displaying the misspelled name "Millenium."[2] From politicians declaring a New World Order to New Agers chanting to herald the Age of Aquarius to Christians proclaiming that the biblical millennium is near, almost everyone eagerly anticipates the year 2000.

In a special issue of *Time* magazine dedicated to the year 2000, Lance Morrow writes: "The world approaches [A.D. 2000] in states of giddiness, expectation and, consciously or unconsciously, a certain anxiety. The millennium looms as civilization's most spectacular birthday, but, as it approaches, the occasion also sends out nagging threats of comeuppance."[3]

Evangelical books on the year 2000 include both fiction works such as Larry Burkett's *The Illuminati* and nonfiction such as Pat Robertson's *The New Millennium*. Robert Van Kampen's bestseller *The Sign,* complete with a colorful end-times chart, announces that for "the first time in 2,000 years the stage is set for the end of the world."[4]

Actually, since the apostles believed they were living in the last days (1 Cor 10:11; 1 Jn 2:18), the stage has been set for almost 2,000 years! Almost every generation of Christians since the first century has believed they were living in the last days. Take the Christians living in A.D. 999. Like our generation, these medieval Christians believed that the signs of their time, including wars, famines, pestilences, immorality and astronomical signs—coupled with rumors such as that Pope Sylvester II was the antichrist—announced the foreboding end in A.D. 1000 (or A.D. 1033, for those who started their countdown from the death of Christ). Many crowded inside and around St. Peter's Basilica in Rome, repenting of their sins. After the midnight bell struck, people cried for joy that no judgment had occurred, and they resumed their normal activities.[5]

Now as A.D. 2000 approaches, soothsayers are once again crying wolf. Prophecy teachers often declare that we are approaching six thousand years of history since the birth of Adam. And reminding us that a day to the Lord is as a thousand years (Ps 90:4; 2 Pet 3:8), they believe that the millennium (Christ's thousand-year reign on earth) will begin around A.D. 2000. (But since the twentieth century really ends on December 31, 2000, some predictors will undoubtedly shoot for that date.) Ray Brubaker, an American promoter of the Korean Hyoo-go movement, declared: "We have had notable men tell us that as God made the world in six days and rested the seventh day, so this world will continue for six thousand years, followed by the Millennium, a time of peace unprecedented in recorded history."[6] A popular end-time tract written by Ron Reese warned that the Great Tribulation might begin in 1992 or 1993 because "*IN 6000 YEARS, THE LORD GOD WILL BRING ALL THINGS TO AN END. . . . The 6000 years are almost over!*"[7]

Most A.D. 2000 calculations find their origin with Bishop James Ussher (1581-1656), an Anglo-Irish prelate who, based on his calculations of biblical genealogies, dated creation at 4004 B.C. How valid are Ussher's date and the day-millennium theory?

Reason 26: If 4004 B.C. Was the Beginning of the World, the End Cannot Take Place in A.D. 2000

Ironically, if Ussher's date is correct, the end cannot take place in the year 2000. If we add six thousand years to 4004 B.C., we arrive somewhere around A.D. 1996 or 1997. Here's the problem: almost every evangelical date-setter believes the rapture will take place before seven years of tribulation. If the end of human history is 1996, then the rapture should have already occurred somewhere between 1989 or 1990.

Prior to 1989, Salem Kirban, author of the *Prophecy Bible* and the bestselling novels *666* and *1000,* suggested a 1989 rapture, faithfully abiding by the precise date of Ussher's chronology.[8] Since then most date-setters have become historical revisionists by rounding off Ussher's formula to 4000 B.C. Those who still accept Ussher's chronology should at least open their eyes and realize that his exact date for the world's creation probably conflicts with their date for the end of the world.

Scaremongers normally calculate their dates for the end based on the Gregorian calendar, which was first implemented in 1582. Prior to that time the Western world used the Julian calendar. When the Gregorian calendar emerged, it advanced the Julian calendar from October 5 to the Gregorian October 15. Since the older calendar was not as precise as the newer, in the thousands-of-years range the Julian calendar would be off by weeks.

Furthermore, from 587 B.C. to A.D. 70 the Jewish world followed a calendar based on a 354-day year, with the addition of a thirteenth month every few years. And from 332 to 200 B.C. the Jews also followed a Macedonian calendar. To complicate matters still further, the Jews had both a civil and a religious calendar.

This hodgepodge of calendars used by the Jews and Christians makes it difficult to calculate precise dates from the beginning of the world to now, as Ussher attempted. There really is no way to affirm that the earth was created in 4004 B.C.—in fact, there is every reason to deny it.

Reason 27: Humans Lived on Earth Prior to 4004 B.C.

Ussher's chronology also does not square with the evidence of history. The earth is older than six thousand years, and numerous people and societies existed before 4004 B.C. This is not some liberal perspective: many conservative scholars—including those who hold to a literal six-day creation (with twenty-four-hour days) in Genesis 1 and 2—openly agree with the evidence that civilizations may have existed before 4004 B.C. And young-earth creation scientists, who affirm that the earth is thousands of years old (as opposed to millions), do not necessarily affirm that the earth was created in 4004 B.C.[9]

The general consensus among scholars is that human civilization dates back about fourteen thousand to thirty-five thousand years with the Les Eyzies and Lascaux cave paintings in France and the Altamira (Spain) Paleolithic paintings (10,000-30,000 B.C.).

Some Civilizations Existing Before 4004 B.C.
Qalat Jarmo (east of Kirkuk, Iraq): 7000 B.C.
Catal Huyuk (in Konya il, Turkey) excavations: 6700-5650 B.C.
Hassuna findings (north Mesopotamia): 5750-5350 B.C.
Tall al-'Ubayd findings (near Ur, Mesopotamia): 5200-3500 B.C.
Badarian era (Egypt): 4000 B.C. (six-thousand-year-old cemeteries were found, indicating that the people were alive prior to 4004 B.C.)

Source: *The New Encyclopaedia Britannica* (Chicago: Encyclopaedia Britannica, 1981).

Reason 28: Genealogies in the Bible Do Not Always List All Ancestors

Tracing back the names listed in the Bible's genealogies (such as those found in Gen 5 and 11, Mt 1 and Lk 3), Ussher arrived at his 4004 B.C. date. But there's one inescapable problem with his method. Biblical genealogies do not always list every descendant (compare Mt 1 to 1 Chron 23:15-16; 26:24; compare Ezra 7:1-5 to 1 Chron 6:3-15). In Scripture, *father* can simply mean "ancestor," while *son* may mean "descendant" (see 2 Kings 16:1-2; Mt 3:9). For instance, Jesus is called the son of David, even though King David lived almost a thousand years before Christ (Mt 1:1). Kings Ahaziah, Joash, Amaziah and Jehoiakim are missing from the genealogy in Matthew 1 (see 1 Chron 3:11-16; 2 Chron 23—25).[10] The Luke 3 genealogy includes the name Cainan (v. 36), but this name is missing from a similar genealogy in Genesis 11:12-13.

Discrepancies within genealogies, however, are not mistakes that somehow disprove the Bible's reliability. Genealogies record ancestral pedigrees, not precise dates and time frames. In some cases certain names were excluded from genealogies for reasons of symmetry—consider the three sets of fourteen names in Matthew 1. Other times people were excluded because of their wicked deeds. At any rate, the genealogies cannot be used to find the correct date for the birth of Adam or the beginning of creation.

The apostle Paul was wise to exhort Christians "not to teach false doctrines any longer nor to devote themselves to myths and endless genealogies. These promote controversies rather than God's work" (1 Tim 1:3-4). Elsewhere he urges, "Avoid foolish controversies and genealogies and arguments and quarrels about the law, because these are unprofitable and useless" (Tit 3:9).

Reason 29: The Predictions of Certain Church Fathers Do Not Justify Date-Setting

Televangelist Jack Van Impe tells us many eminent church fathers believed the world would last six thousand years before Christ returned; he claims that their predictions point to the year 2000. Among the most prominent of the Christian leaders he cites are Barnabas, Irenaeus, Hippolytus and Martin Luther.[11]

It is true that Martin Luther believed the time of the end was near. But it seems unlikely that he believed the end would occur in A.D. 2000. He also claimed the date of Christ's coming lay "hid in God of which we know nothing."[12] In his view, Christians cannot know the precise time of the end any more than an infant in its mother's womb can know when it will be born.[13]

Virtually all scholars agree that the Epistle of Barnabas was not written by the same Barnabas who was the companion of Paul. It is sometimes even called Pseudo-Barnabas.[14] But the myth of Barnabas's end-time prophesies continues to be taught and publicized, even in full-page ads in the *Los Angeles Times*.[15] The author of the Epistle of Barnabas did hold to six thousand years of history, but there is no evidence that he believed doomsday would fall on A.D. 2000. The same holds true for Irenaeus. Bishop Ussher did not even propose his 4004 B.C. date until the seventeenth century; Irenaeus lived in the third century A.D.

Hippolytus, who was influenced by Irenaeus, believed Christ would return six thousand years after Adam, but he believed Christ's birth was fifty-five hundred years after Adam (*On Daniel* 2.4). It seems that some of the church fathers (including Hippolytus, Irenaeus and Lactantius) believed the Second Coming would occur around A.D. 500.[16] Other early church writers, however, did not indulge in date-setting, but confessed with Jesus and the apostles that no one knew when the Lord would return (see *Didache* 16.1; *Hermas Visions* 3.8.9; Jerome *Against Jovinianus* 2.25). In general, the early church believed the day of the Lord's return was veiled.[17]

But even if some well-known Christians in times past believed the end would take place in A.D. 2000, this does not mean they were right! Humans make mistakes, but Scripture does not make a mistake when it warns us that no one knows the time of Christ's return (Mk 13:32; Acts 1:7).

Reason 30: Scripture Does Not Say That Christ Will Return by A.D. 2000

On the *Praise the Lord* show hosted by Paul and Jan Crouch, founders of the massive Trinity Broadcasting Network, Joseph Good, president of Hatikva Ministries, affirmed that the rapture will definitely occur by the year 2000. His reason? He points out that Hosea 6:2 and John 2:19 speak of being raised on the third day. If one assumes that a day represents a thousand years (2 Pet 3:8), these passages hint that in the third "day" from the time of Christ (A.D. 2000-3000), the end will take place.[18]

Arno Froese, president of Midnight Call Ministries (reportedly the largest biblical prophetic ministry in the world), teaches that Exodus

19:10-11 shows another example of how God's people will meet God after three days, as does the wedding feast of Cana (Jn 1:51—2:11). Moreover, conflating the views of Ussher and Joachim of Fiore (a medieval soothsayer), Froese divides history into three segments—two thousand years without the Law (of Moses), two thousand years under the Law, and two thousand years under grace, which, of course, will end about A.D. 2000.[19]

Actually, the Law of Moses was written about 1400 B.C., so Abraham is sometimes a substitute for Moses within the Law era. Still, Abraham was probably born somewhere between 2100 and 2200 B.C., so he does not properly fit this model either. This shows how arbitrary prophecy divisions can be. A plain reading of John 1:51—2:11 and Exodus 19 shows these passages to be historical narratives. God never intended them to be interpreted in such a way that they would give us a hidden date for the end. It's interesting how prophetic teachers—who almost universally read literal meanings into highly symbolic prophecy texts—are now reading symbolic meanings into literal narratives.

Moreover, Hosea 6:2 does not point to A.D. 2000. In this passage Hosea appeals to the Israelites to repent of their wicked ways. If they did so, even though the enemy (Assyria) had devastated them, God would raise the Israelites on "the third day." Here "the third day" represents a short period of time. In other words, God would *quickly* restore a repentant Israel (compare Deut 32:39; Amos 1:3). This has nothing to do with the Second Coming of Christ two thousand years after his birth.[20] And the Israelites, like Orthodox Jews today, did not follow a Christian calendar, so our two-thousand-year measurements bear no significance to them.[21]

Furthermore, the point of 2 Peter 3:8 is not that one day in God's time registers as a thousand years in our time. Although the verse does affirm that a day to the Lord is as a thousand years, it also states that a thousand years is as a day. The point is simply that God's timing is not our timing (compare Is 55:8). What we may consider long God may consider short; and what we consider short God may consider intensely long.

The end could come at any moment, or thousands of years in the future. We simply don't know, because God's timing is not ours.

6
Reasons Why
No One
Can Know the Date
Through the Signs
of the Times

*T*he vision of street preacher John Gunter: on May 3, 1993, Portland, Oregon, would be destroyed by a great earthquake because of its demonic activities.[1] Gordon-Michael Scallion, another soothsayer, predicted that 1993 would be "the Year of the Great Earthquakes." California was destined for devastation, and the Golden Gate Bridge would suffer damage.[2] Prophecy speculators tell us that earthquakes are just one of many omens warning the end has come.

Jesus said that as we approach the last days,
> many will come in my name, claiming, "I am he," and, "The time is near." Do not follow them. When you hear of wars and revolutions, do not be frightened. These things must happen first, but the end will not come right away. . . . Nation will rise against nation,

and kingdom against kingdom. There will be great earthquakes, famines and pestilences in various places, and fearful events and great signs from heaven. (Lk 21:8-11)

These prophetic verses speak of apostasy and false Christs, great wars, killer earthquakes, the spread of famine and pestilence, and fearful signs in the sky. These are reportedly the signs of end times, which become incentives for setting end-time dates. Is this legitimate?

Reason 31: The Change of Weather Patterns Does Not Indicate That the End Will Come in Our Lifetime

He preached across the street from my church, crying out that sinners like our church members should repent because Judgment Day was around the corner. Strangely, this wild-eyed young man was preaching to the church he had once attended. He waved a newspaper with headlines that screamed "Farmers Blame God for Lack of Rain." The Midwestern drought in the late 1980s had convinced him that the end had arrived.

But the Bible does not directly connect changes in weather patterns with the coming of the end. Doomsday advocates cite Luke 21:25: "There will be signs in the sun, moon and stars. On the earth, nations will be in anguish and perplexity at the roaring and tossing of the sea." This passage might not even refer to future changes in the weather. "The roaring and tossing of the sea" may figuratively signify tumult among the nations (compare Is 17:12; Rev 17:15). If we take Revelation 16:8-9 literally, people may get scorched with great heat during the last days. But this will not happen until the very last judgments on earth, immediately preceding the Lord's defeat of the Beast.

Still, we do hear reports about global warming. Certain climatologists claim the earth is generally getting warmer. Over the process of many years, global warming may melt the great polar ice caps and thus cause severe changes in the weather.

Weather trends are very difficult to predict because of their chaotic nature. Forecasters often fail to predict next week's weather accurately; and it is much *more* difficult to predict a major weather trend years in advance.

Global warming advocates sometimes forget that clouds can both warm the earth by 9 degrees Fahrenheit and cool it by about 22 degrees.[3] Nature appears to have a built-in adjuster, so clouds could prevent extreme warming of the earth. And God, the sustainer of our planet, has so ordained it (Col 1:16-17; Heb 1:3). When promising Noah that he would never again flood the entire earth, God also promised: "As long as the earth endures, seedtime and harvest, cold and heat, summer and winter, day and night will never cease" (Gen 8:22).

Reason 32: Wars and Rumors of Wars Are Not Sufficient to Tell Us the Time of the End

Have you ever heard prophecy teachers proclaim that the Bible predicts helicopters containing stun guns, based on the locusts with scorpion tails that "torment people for five months" in Revelation 9:3-10? Or how about how the A-bomb set off at Bikini Island in the 1940s was the "huge mountain, all ablaze" in Revelation 8:8? What about how the 1986 Chernobyl nuclear disaster in Russia fulfilled the prophecy of Wormwood-induced bitterness of waters in Revelation 8:10-11? The positive "proof" of the latter: Chernobyl means "wormwood" in Ukrainian.[4]

Such images allegedly fit the warning Jesus gave concerning wars and rumors of wars as signs of the end times. A critical reading of Revelation 8—9, however, reveals the shortcomings of these alleged prophecy fulfillments. Chernobyl, for instance, is the name of a Ukrainian city, not a "star" that falls from heaven to earth as portrayed in Revelation 8:10-11. Prophetic teachers almost uniformly stress literalistic interpretation of Scripture, but they generally feel free to switch to symbolic interpretation whenever it seems to support their wild speculations.

Still, the military capacity of today's world has an unprecedented gravity. We now have the capacity to destroy the earth through a nuclear holocaust. Grant Jeffrey writes: "Never before in the history of the world have there been so many wars and rumors of wars; and never before has there been so much potential for total destruction."[5] In 1975, he says, "nuclear and political scientists from Massachusetts Institute of Technology and Harvard University" met to discuss the possibility of nuclear war and concluded that one would definitely occur before A.D. 2000.[6]

Is nuclear warfare inevitable by the year 2000? Nuclear hype prevails not only among prophecy teachers but also among certain secular celebrities. Both Edgar Whisenant and Carl Sagan warn us about the consequences of a nuclear "winter" in which the sun's rays would not be able to reach the earth because of nuclear smoke clouds. Whisenant claims this could cause worldwide temperatures to drop as much as 104 degrees Fahrenheit.[7] But these holocaust scenarios are blown out of proportion. "Nuclear autumn" better describes the consequences of all-out nuclear warfare. If such a holocaust did occur, temperatures might not drop at all but actually rise.[8] At most, one scientist claims, the temperature would drop only 25 degrees.[9] The fact that a group of scientists back in 1975 could not see peace beyond twenty-five years does not seal our fate. The entire geopolitical situation has drastically changed since 1975. This is why Jeffrey had to cite a conference held almost twenty years earlier. The same scientists today probably do not even agree with the conclusions they reached in 1975.

Are wars on the increase? World War I and II are generally thought of as the most devastating of all wars. There have been other wars, however, that were just as horrendous. The Thirty Years' War (1618-1648), the Manchu-Chinese War (1644) and the Taiping Rebellion (1850-1864) claimed the lives of tens of millions, just like the two world wars.

When people claim that more wars and casualties of war have occurred in the twentieth century than in earlier times, we need to remember that many more people have lived in the twentieth century than at any earlier century. *Proportionally,* in fact, wars in previous centuries wrought greater devastation. Moreover, the number of wars did not increase during the twentieth century. Quincy Wright, a pioneer researcher in the history of warfare, defines a war as a battle involving at least fifty thousand soldiers. From 1480 to 1964, an average of sixty wars of this magnitude were fought per century, but there were only thirty from 1900 to 1964.[10] It is better to understand war as a perpetual sign of the final age that began in the first century A.D.

Reason 33: Current Famines Do Not Tell Us the Time of the End

By the year 2000, world population will rise to about six billion, as world resources dwindle. Environmentalist exponent Paul Ehrlich predicts that by 1999 there will be a famine in the United States in which millions will starve to death.[11] Famine is another sign of the end times. We see famine in Somalia and other parts of the world, but do such famines indicate that the end is at hand?

First, we need to make an often-neglected distinction between starvation and malnutrition. About one billion people suffer from malnutrition, while starvation afflicts forty million—only about 1 percent of the total human population. Actually, famines decreased in the twentieth century in relation to earlier times. In the nineteenth century, the Irish Potato Famine claimed the lives of one million Europeans (1846-1847). This seems minor, however, in comparison to China's famine in the same century—a tragedy that claimed the lives of approximately 100 million![12]

If Christians are really concerned about famines, instead of buying speculative end-time books they should donate some of their finances to those who are less fortunate.

Reason 34: Current Pestilences Do Not Tell Us the Time of the End

"Noisome pestilence" and "terror by night" in Psalm 91 (KJV) are references to the AIDS epidemic. By 1991 everyone would know someone with AIDS, according to J. R. Church.[13] The end-time sign of pestilence has finally arrived with AIDS, "the worst plague in history," which increases by 20 percent each year, according to Noah Hutchings of Southwest Radio Church.[14]

AIDS is a tragic condition. Devastating as it is, however, the spread of AIDS does not necessarily prove the end will take place in a few more years. The world has seen at least one worse pestilence—the Black Plague of the fourteenth century. Along the trade routes of Europe, this plague killed about one out of every three persons.[15] The poet Giovanni Boccaccio, who lived in that fearful time, described the tumors caused by the plague. They lodged in the groin or under the armpit and grew to the size of an egg or an apple. After these symptoms appeared, "almost all died within three days."[16]

Russell Chandler, former religion writer for the *Los Angeles Times,* offers this further description:

> The disease apparently spread to Europe via a ship filled with refugees from the Crimea. Passengers already stricken with the Black Death disembarked in Sicily. So did the hosts of rats and their millions of fleas that—physicians were to discover five centuries later—carried the disease. By the beginning of the fifteenth century, the plague had killed up to forty million Europeans. Some regions lost as much as three-quarters of their population and some parts of England up to nine-tenths. Europe soon ran out of "pickmen"—paid to bury the dead—and "bodies were tossed into huge overflowing trenches or left to rot in the streets where they would be torn apart by dogs."[17]

Reason 35: Current Earthquakes Do Not Tell Us the Time of the End

Larry Wilson, a former Seventh-day Adventist pastor, predicted four massive global earthquakes beginning around 1994 and ending in 1998 with the Second Coming.[18] Earthquake predictions are nothing new. In

1984 Peter and Beverly Caruso, Assembly of God ministers, predicted that a major earthquake would rock Southern California during the summer Olympic Games. Al Dager, editor of *Media Spotlight,* wrote on their behalf: "If they're wrong they are risking an entire lifetime of ministry to be called false prophets. The risk on their part should at least cause us to listen."[19] That summer, Southern Californians waited for the big one, but it never came. Major earthquakes that *have* hit California—such as the San Francisco (October 1989) and Los Angeles (January 1994) shakes—were not predicted by such date-setters.

Other doomsday advocates believe earthquakes are a sign of the end because they are increasing drastically. Jack Van Impe claims that twenty-four major earthquakes took place from the time of Christ to 1950, but that over thirty-one major shakers have come since 1950.[20] Prophetic writer Robert W. Faid claims the number of deaths caused by earthquakes increased by 900 percent in the twentieth century.[21]

But reliable statistics show that earthquakes have not increased in the twentieth century. The only thing that has increased is our ability to detect them. The first proper seismograph was not even developed until 1880. Also, existing earthquake records prior to the eighteenth century are almost entirely confined to southern Europe, Japan and China. There is no way of knowing how many killer quakes devastated continents such as Africa, Australia and the Americas prior to this time.

Those who preach distorted earthquake statistics get their information from sources that give an incomplete picture of major earthquakes.[22] John Milne, the father of modern seismology, lists a total of 4,151 devastating earthquakes from A.D. 7 to A.D. 1899.[23] In fact, more people died between 1715 and 1783 from earthquakes (1,373,845) than between 1915 and 1983 (1,210,597).[24] Moreover, when we compare figures from 1900 with figures from 1990, both major (8.0 magnitude or higher) and shallow (7.0 magnitude and higher) earthquakes have declined in number and global energy (energy released from earthquakes); see figure 1.

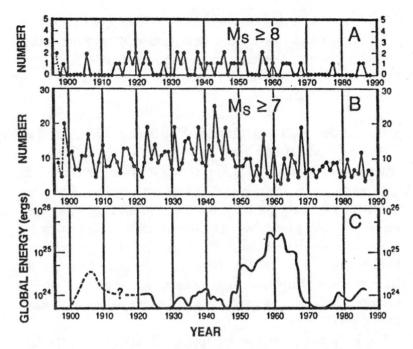

A. Number of great earthquakes with measured surface wave magnitudes greater than or equal to 8.0 reported each year since 1897.
B. Number of shallow earthquakes with surface wave magnitudes greater than or equal to 7.0 reported each year since 1897.
C. Global energy of large earthquakes assembled from seismograph records beginning with the year 1900. Curve shows five-year running average (in ergs per year) displayed on the logarithmic energy scale.

Figure 1. Global summary of ninety years of seismograph records showing the frequency and energy of large shallow earthquakes. (First published in Steven A. Austin's "Earthquakes in These Last Days," *Impact* [Institute for Creation Research], December 1989. Used by permission.)

Charles F. Richter, inventor of the Richter Scale, states:

One notices with some amusement that certain religious groups have picked this rather unfortunate time to insist that the number of earthquakes is increasing. In part they are misled by the increasing number of small earthquakes that are being catalogued and listed by newer, more sensitive stations throughout the world. It is worth remarking that the number of great [that is, 8.0 and over on the Richter scale] earthquakes from 1896 to 1906 (about twenty-five) *was greater than in any ten-year interval since.*[25]

Earthquake figures proclaimed by doomsday advocates do not square with the actual facts.

Reason 36: Environmental Problems Do Not Tell Us the Time of the End

Environmentalists often point to such things as the depletion of the rain forests and the thinning of the ozone layer as signs of a coming doomsday that can be prevented only if humankind adopts their agenda—which, among nonbelieving environmentalists, is often New Age in orientation.[26] With holes in the ozone layer—which protects us from excessive radiation from the sun—we are told we could suffer more severe sunburns and more cases of skin cancer. A growing number of scientists and laypeople, however, are willing to challenge these views.[27]

The Bible prophesies that the forests will remain until the final judgments of God destroy the earth. And they will not be destroyed by lumberjacks, but by fire (Rev 7:1-3; 8:7; 11:18). Nevertheless, this does not give us license to "rape" the land. Careless logging and "slash-and-burn" farming could still cause great damage to our forests.

The recent thinning of the ozone layer—supposedly caused by refrigerants known as chlorofluorocarbons (CFCs)—has simply reduced the layer back to its level prior to the 1960s, when it increased by 5 percent. It is possible that there is no true depletion, only a leveling off from excess thickness accumulated within the last few decades. Even if there is a current depletion, studies confirm that the ozone layer naturally heals itself.[28] What's more, there would be no ill effects from UV (ultraviolet) leakage even if the ozone layer were reduced by 20 percent.[29] There definitely seem to be holes in the ozone theory.

Yet Christians should not cover their ears to calls to protect God's creation. We have a responsibility to be good stewards of the earth.

If some people abuse prophecy in connection with ecology, this does not give us the right to abuse the earth. We should avoid two extremes: (1) assuming that the world will be completely destroyed through our environmental negligence and (2) asserting that our negligence does not do any significant damage to the environment.

Reason 37: Signs in the Sky Are Not Sufficient to Tell Us the Time of the End

In 1982 the alignment of planets in our solar system was supposed to cause a gravitational pull that would trigger killer earthquakes and change weather patterns. Prophecy teachers such as Hal Lindsey, Pat Robertson, David Webber and Wim Malgo heralded this end-time alignment, called the Jupiter Effect. Yet the planets aligned in 1982 with no devastating consequences. More threatening was an asteroid half a mile long that missed the earth by a mere 700,000 miles on March 23, 1989. Another comet called the Swift Tuttle might get too close to the earth in A.D. 2126. Donald Yeoman of NASA said, "Sooner or later, our planet will be struck by one of them [a comet or asteroid]."[30]

Signs of the time? Actually, comets have hit the earth before. The last big one struck Siberia on June 30, 1908, wiping out thousands of square miles of forest.

Reginald Dunlop, editor of *End-Times News & Prophecy Digest,* claims that the "shaken" heavenly bodies of Mark 13:25 are actually falling hydrogen bombs, which will be "THE SIGN FOR TIME OF NUCLEAR WAR COMING BEFORE FALL 1994."[31]

Adding a new twist to the theme of signs from heaven, Jack Van Impe claims the mysterious crop circles that have appeared in fields around the world may be an end-time sign from the skies (see Lk 21:11).[32] These circles—which flatten crops in a swirling design sometimes thirty-six feet wide or wider—are sometimes attributed to UFOs. In September 1991 two British men, David Chorley and Doug Bower, confessed they were the culprits behind this hoax. Although this phenomenon appears around the globe, one writer suggests: "The intelligent lifeforms that created the 750 cryptic crop circles worldwide most likely are farmers or their teen-age kids, who are laughing their overalls off right now."[33]

But even if we have no definitive explanation for the crop circles, it doesn't follow that these designs are "signs from heaven." We can assume this only if we've already assumed that the circles are caused by UFOs. When Jesus spoke of "signs from heaven," however, he was referring to "signs in the sun, moon and stars," not UFOs (see Lk 21:11, 25).

Even if these crop circles were indeed signs of the end times, this still would not settle how close we are to the end. Crop circles have troubled farmers from as early as 1678![34] We can safely affirm that eclipses, comets, UFOs and other signs from the sky are insufficient for date-setting.

Reason 38: The Current Increase of Apostasy and Sin Does Not Tell Us the Date of the End

"In the last days," the apostle Paul writes,

> people will be lovers of themselves, lovers of money, boastful, proud, abusive, disobedient to their parents, ungrateful, unholy, without love, unforgiving, slanderous, without self-control, brutal, not lovers of the good, treacherous, rash, conceited, lovers of pleasure rather than lovers of God—having a form of godliness but denying its power. Have nothing to do with them. (2 Tim 3:2-5)

Without a doubt, today's world fits this description. Fornication, abortion, drug abuse, crime, gangs and child abuse are all-too-common indicators of our culture's immorality. Jesus predicted that there would be a proliferation of false prophets who would deceive many (Mt 24:4-5, 23-25), and indeed apostate cults have flourished in the twentieth century, led by infamous false prophets such as Jim Jones, the Reverend Sun Myung Moon and David Koresh.

Before we assume too much, however, we need to understand that

Scripture is not speaking of the last days as some remote era in the future, but as the very days of the apostles. This is the impact of the often-ignored command that comes at the end of 2 Timothy 3:5: "Have nothing to do with them." Paul was exhorting Timothy to stay away from the sinful activities that characterized the corrupt sinful nature of humans living in the final era—an era that has now lasted almost two thousand years. Paul's description fits our generation so perfectly because it fits sinful human nature in general. Since the time of Paul, has such a description *not* fit humankind? There have been sinful humans and false prophets ever since the first century. Furthermore, both Scripture and the first-century Jewish historian Josephus give accounts of many false messiahs who led many astray (Acts 5:36-37; 8:9-10; *Wars* 2.13).

Harold Camping claims the entire church is becoming apostate. This is his foremost sign that we are living in the final tribulation.[35] Although we hear about many cults and apostate liberals, the notion of a mass Christian apostasy does not reflect current statistics. As I noted in an earlier chapter, many of the baby boomers who fell away from the churches in the 1960s are now returning. Just from 1991 to 1992, the number of Americans who said they value the Bible very highly increased by 8 percent among baby busters (persons born between 1964 and 1982), 10 percent among baby boomers (those born from 1946 to 1964) and 17 percent among those between ages 46-64. In 1986, 48 percent of American adults could be found in church in a given week. This percentage has fluctuated slightly, going down to 43 percent in 1988, but by 1991 it had risen again to 49 percent. Also, 40 percent of Americans claim to be born again.[36]

Now of course I cannot vouch for all those who claim to be born again and to attend church regularly. Some may have a wrong concept of the born-again experience. Some may attend church without truly being converted. Still, we cannot deny that many of these Americans are genuine believers. For instance, 40 percent of the church attenders had shared their faith with someone else in the past month, and this percentage has not changed significantly during the last several years.[37] And when we look beyond the United States, we find there are millions of people converting to Christianity from Africa, South America, and Russia and other former communist countries.

Still, regardless of statistics, sin runs rampant in our society. What can the Christian do to alleviate the problem? Instead of merely pointing to the sinful state of the world as an end-time sign, why not reach out to lost people with the hope-filled truth of Christ? Unregenerate sinners—whether criminals, political leaders, prostitutes, gang members, drug addicts, cultists, skeptics or homosexuals—are still human beings created in God's image who think, feel, hurt and need our love. We should not write them off as hopeless pawns of the antichrist ready to be devoured by the fires of Armageddon. No matter how close we are to the end, there's still hope for the most wretched sinner, and Jesus is still the answer for a dying world (2 Pet 3:9).

Reason 39: The Increase in Technology Does Not Indicate the Date of the End

A little tract distributed by Osterhus Publishing House in Minneapolis offers a list of signs of the last days. According to this tract, among the last-day signs predicted by Scripture are automobiles (Nahum 2:3-4) and aircraft (Is 31:5; 60:8).[38] Inventions created by human knowledge have definitely increased in dramatic proportions in the last century. Some of our grandparents and great-grandparents can recall a world without cars, television, jets, helicopters and rockets. Many of the rest of us can recall living without computers, videos, push-button phones and microwave ovens.

Daniel 12:4 predicts that knowledge will increase as we approach the end. But *how much* increase in knowledge must occur before the end? This we cannot know.

End-time soothsayers often fail to notice Christ's reassuring words about the signs of the end: "You will hear of wars and rumors of wars, but see to it that you are not alarmed. Such things must happen, *but the end is still to come"* (Mt 24:6; compare Lk 21:8-11). The signs are merely the beginning of birth pangs that will reach their completion during the end times (Mt 24:8). *They characterize the entire church era.*

Around 200 A.D., the church father Tertullian pointed to the very same signs of the end, as did Pope Gregory in the sixth century and believers in the fourteenth century and many others. We will continue to see such signs as we get closer to the end, but they in no way indicate how close we are to the end.

In Luke 17:20 the Lord affirms that we cannot know or predict by external observations the time of the end. Christ's Second Coming will be sudden and unexpected (Lk 17:22-37). The Greek word for observation *(paratērēsis)* appears only in Luke 17:20. In other Greek literature the word can refer to the observation of signs in the sky. One Bible commentary assures us this passage indicates that "there will be no such signs as would enable a watcher to date the arrival."[39]

7
Reasons Why No One Knows the Date Through Current World Affairs

*T*he ark of the covenant has been found! According to a legend from the Royal Chronicles kept by priests in Ethiopia, when the Ethiopian Queen of Sheba visited King Solomon the two rulers made love. Eventually the Queen of Sheba gave birth to Solomon's son, Menelik I Solomon. When the boy was nineteen, he prepared to return to Ethiopia from Jerusalem. Solomon gave his son a replica of the ark of the covenant, but at the young man's farewell banquet the Hebrew priests got drunk, and Menelik managed to steal the real ark and substitute the replica. To this day the ark remains hidden in an ancient church in Aksum-Aduwa, Ethiopia.[1] Once the ark is publicly revealed, it will supposedly be transported to the Jewish temple, which is currently being rebuilt. The Jews will then resume temple sacrifices—a sign of the final countdown to the end.

But there are some insurmountable problems with this report. First, the Bible nowhere hints that Solomon had sex with the Queen of Sheba (see 1 Kings 10). Second, if Solomon had made a duplicate ark, he would no doubt have been punished by God as was Jeroboam, who established a worship site that rivaled the temple in Jerusalem (1 Kings 12:25—13:6). Third, only the high priest could enter into the Holy of Holies, the inner chamber of the temple where the ark was located. If anyone touched the ark who was not designated to carry it, he would have been killed (Ex 19:22; 1 Sam 6:1-8).

Fourth, the original ark was still in Jerusalem during the reign of Josiah, hundreds of years after Solomon (2 Chron 35:3). Finally, if the ark is hidden in an Ethiopian church, why has no one seen it? This would indeed be the greatest archaeological find of the twentieth century, perhaps of all time. Grant Jeffrey, who promotes this legend from Ethiopia—the blessed land that harbors the true ark—nevertheless condemns Ethiopia as one of the wicked nations that, along with Russia ("Gog and Magog"), will attack Israel.[2]

Prophetic teachers often mistakenly tie current nations or world events into their end-time schemes. The danger with this type of end-time speculation is fourfold. First, it encourages misguided teachers to set dates for the end. Second, it maligns the character of the people, organizations or nations that are castigated as end-time monsters by evangelicals. Third, when speculations are preached as though they were biblical "facts" and are then proved wrong, this gives unbelievers one more excuse for rejecting Christianity. Fourth, such speculations consume our time and money, leading us into a fruitless and disappointing endeavor that distracts us from our commitment to influence the world. Let's examine some of the most popular among such claims.

Reason 40: The Fact That Israel Has Returned to Palestine Does Not Necessarily Mean That Christ Will Return in Our Generation

WHAT COULD HAPPEN IN THE YEAR STARTING IN MAY 1987? COULD THERE BE A PRE-TRIBULATION RAPTURE

OF THE SAINTS BY MAY 1988? COULD WORLD WAR NUMBER THREE WITH THE SOVIET UNION AND THE STATE OF ISRAEL START? . . . and above all . . . WILL THIS ERA OF TIME *START GOD'S CLOCK OF PROPHECY TICK-ING FOR ISRAEL AGAIN, AS PREDICTED IN DANIEL 9:24-27?* THERE IS NO DOUBT THAT WE WHO BELIEVE IN THE LORD JESUS CHRIST ARE SEEING THE ENDING OF THE FORTY YEAR GENERATION AND THE BEGINNING OF THE COUNTDOWN TO THE COMING OF JESUS CHRIST.[3]

This is how Doug Clark's book begins. Clark hosted his own program, *Final Shockwaves to Armageddon,* on Paul Crouch's Trinity Broadcasting Network before he skipped town. He is now on the Postal Inspection Service's wanted list for mail fraud. Like Clark, many prophecy buffs would have us believe that the Jews' return to Palestine in 1948 marked the beginning of the last generation.

In a recent interview in Peter and Patti Lalonde's *This Week in Bible Prophecy,* Hal Lindsey stated his position:

I have believed from the beginning when I started studying prophecy thirty-eight years ago that the generation of the fig tree that Jesus talked about in Matthew 24 was the generation that would see all the signs come together, and that would be the generation that would see the return of Christ. I haven't changed; I believe that is happening right now. This is the generation that will see the coming of the Lord.[4]

When asked how long a generation lasts, Lindsey's answer becomes vague. He suggests that a generation could be forty years from Israel's 1967 occupation of Jerusalem, or perhaps a hundred years from 1948.[5] These suggestions are still problematic, because even with his broadest definition of a generation, Lindsey is implicitly setting a date: at the very latest, Christ will return by A.D. 2048.

Flexibility, by the way, works to date-setters' advantage. If a calculation based on 1948 fails, they can always set another date based on the 1993 peace accord, or Israel's occupation of Jerusalem in 1967, or the Balfour Declaration in 1917. M. J. Agee claims that forty years from 1967 (at noon on September 13, 2007), an asteroid will hit this planet, knocking it upside-down. This will happen concurrent with a second rapture, and then Christ will return on April 6, 2008.[6]

Jack Van Impe averages out a generation to 47.523 years, based on the number of generations in Matthew 1 (forty-two in all). He adds these years to 1948 to arrive at 1996. If that prediction fails, Van Impe reserves a follow-up scheme by dividing the forty-two generations by 2,166 years (the number of years between Abraham and Christ) to get 51.5 years. This number is added to 1948 to suggest 1999 as another possible date for the end.[7] James T. Harmon, another prophetic teacher, added 51.57 years to May 15, 1949—the date the United Nations recognized Israel's national identity—and subtracted 7 (the years of the tribulation) to suggest a 1993 rapture. In case that date didn't work, he reserved 1996, 2012 and 2022 as backup dates![8]

These calculations, ingenious as they seem, are nothing new. Medieval sage Joachim of Fiore used the forty-two generations in Matthew 1 to describe an entire era he called the Age of Grace. Assuming an average generation to be thirty years, Joachim multiplied the forty-two generations by thirty to predict the end in A.D. 1260.[9]

The two most crucial questions surrounding Israel's return to Palestine relate to the interpretation of Matthew 24:32-34: (1) Does the fig tree that Jesus mentions represent Israel? (2) What did Christ mean when he said that "this generation" would not pass until all "these things" were fulfilled?

1. The fig tree in Matthew 24:32-34 does not represent Israel. Clearly, we cannot discover the nation of Israel hidden among the leaves of every fig tree mentioned in Scripture. Sometimes a fig tree represents peace and prosperity (1 Kings 4:25; Mic 4:4); sometimes it's just a plain old fig tree! In fact, there is no indication that Jesus intended his apostles to discern a secret reference to any particular nation in Matthew 24:32-34. In the parallel passage in Luke, Jesus says, "Look at the fig tree *and all the trees.* When they sprout leaves, you can see for yourselves and know that summer [the time] is near" (Lk 21:29-30). Since at the time he was sitting on the Mount of Olives (see Mt 24:2-3)—famous for its fig trees—he simply selected the fig tree as an end-time illustration because it was the most immediate object lesson available.

In one reference where scholars suggest the fig tree *does* represent Israel (Mk 11:12-14, 20-21; compare Mt 21:18-20), Jesus curses the tree so that it can never again bear fruit. He was saying that Israel was spiritually dead. It is difficult to imagine that Israel, as a nation, is once again represented by the fig tree in Matthew 24:32-34 when Jesus has just cursed the nation forever in Matthew 21:18-20.

This leads to another important point. Biblical prophecies regarding the return of the Jews to Palestine (such as Jer 32; Ezek 37; Is 11) universally speak of God's blessing on them, but these passages are all referring to the millennium (the thousand-year reign of Messiah on earth). In any case, how can the Jews have returned to Palestine with God's prophetic blessing when they still reject Jesus as their Messiah? *God's acceptance of the Jews entails not their repossession of the Holy Land, but their acceptance of Jesus as their Messiah* (Mt 21:33-44; 22:1-14; 23; Lk 14:15-24). It is more reasonable to believe that the Jews have forever forfeited their prophetic blessings and divinely given right to Palestine *unless* they recognize Jesus as their Messiah.

2. The "generation" that would see the signs was the first-century saints. The phrase "this generation" in Matthew 24:34 does not refer to our generation, which has seen Israel return to Palestine in 1948. It refers to the Jews living in the first century. The signs they would see are mentioned in the parallel accounts of Matthew 24, Mark 13 and Luke 21, which, when compared, do not necessarily depict a chronological sequence of events.[10] After Christ prophesied that the temple would be destroyed (Mt 24:1-3; Mk 13:1-4; Lk 21:5-7), the disciples asked him at least two distinct questions: (1) When would "these things" (that is, the events leading up to the destruction of the temple in A.D. 70) come to pass? (2) What would be the sign of his coming and of the end of the age?

Jesus answers the first question in Matthew 24:4-28 (compare Mk 13:5-23; Lk 21:8-24) and the second question in Matthew 24:29-31 (compare Mk 13:24-27; Lk 21:25-28). He then refers back to the events leading up to the destruction of the temple when he gives the parable of the fig tree (Mt 24:32-35; Mk 13:28-31; Lk 21:29-33). The statement "This *generation* will certainly not pass away until *all these things* have happened" refers to the first-century Jews who would see the signs in Matthew 24:4-28 (compare Mt 16:28; 23:35-39; Mk 8:12, 38; 9:19).

Notice the change of persons being addressed. Jesus originally uses the second-person plural pronoun, *you,* in connection with the events leading up to the destruction of the temple. *You* is also used in connection with the signs mentioned in the parable of the fig tree. But then *you* changes to the third-person plural, *they,* when Jesus speaks of the events leading to his return (Mt 24:29-31). The disciples were expected to live to see the events leading up to the destruction of the temple in A.D. 70, spoken of in the parable of the fig tree, but they were not expected to see Christ's return.

Those living in the first century experienced the wars, famines, earthquakes, pestilences, false Christs, persecutions and tribulations mentioned in these passages. Other parts of the New Testament tell us of false prophets and messiahs such as Theudas, Judas the Galilean and Elymas in the first century (Acts 5:34-37; 13:4-12). Many false teachers infiltrated the church (2 Cor 11; Gal 1:6-10; 2 Pet 2; Jude 4). Earthquakes were abundant (Acts 16:26; Josephus *Wars* 4.4.5), as were famines, persecutions and other signs (Acts 8:1-4; 11:27-29; 12:1-23; Rom 15:25-28; 1 Cor 16:1-5). Such calamities are confirmed by writings of non-Christian historians of the day such as Suetonius, Tacitus and Josephus.[11]

This explains how Christ could say he had revealed "everything" to his disciples (Mk 13:23), yet years later he revealed more of the future to them in the book of Revelation. Is this a contradiction? No. He revealed "everything" specifically in regard to the events leading to the temple's destruction in A.D. 70. These were predicted in Mark 13:5-23, 28-31. And as recorded in Mark 13:24-27, 32-37, Jesus also told his followers some things about his Second Coming, but there was still more he needed to reveal about this; so *after* A.D. 70 (Revelation was written around A.D. 95) he gave the apostle John more information about his return and the events preceding it.

Jim Stafford's way of outlining the Mount Olivet discourse is helpful:[12]

	Matthew 24	Mark 13	Luke 21
Occasion of the address	1-3	1-4	5-7
Warnings against being led astray by false prophets or calamities	4-8	5-8	8-11
Persecution foretold and help promised	9-14	9-13	12-19
Destruction of Jerusalem and dispersion of Jews	15-28	14-23	20-24
The coming of Christ	29-31	24-27	25-28
Watching for events of this generation leading to the judgment on Jerusalem	32-35	28-31	29-33
Watching for the coming of Christ	36-51	32-37	34-36

Once we understand "this generation" to be first-century believers, it solves the problem of how the disciples were expected to be able to know when the time was near—even "right at the door" (Mt 24:32-34)—but not to be able to know when Jesus would return as a thief in the night (Mt 24:36-44). The parable of the fig tree in Matthew 24:32-34 was told for those living in the first century regarding the destruction of the temple, but the thief-in-the-night lesson refers to Christ's return and is also given to subsequent generations.[13]

Reason 41: The Temple in Jerusalem Is Not Currently Being Rebuilt

A Jewish group called the Temple Institute is currently making vessels that will be used in the new temple. Talmudic schools and Jewish sects such as the Temple Mount Faithful teach students how to perform temple rituals involving animal sacrifices. A computer stores a detailed genealogy allegedly tracing back Levitical lineages to Aaron, the first high priest. Rabbi Kahane, who preserves these lists of qualified priests—complete with names and addresses—believes he will see the Messiah very soon and will present him the list, saying, "Here, Mr. Messiah, is your database!"[14]

This is the current preparation status for the rebuilding of the temple in Jerusalem—which was originally destroyed in 587 B.C. by the Babylonians, rebuilt after the Jews returned to Jerusalem several decades later, and then destroyed again in A.D. 70 by the Romans. We are told by Woody Young and Chuck Missler, "Preparation for the Third Temple is well under way."[15]

But such preparations do not necessarily mean the temple will soon be rebuilt. Reports that Israel is now stockpiling limestone to rebuild the temple in Jerusalem are simply rumors. If you have visited Jerusalem lately, you have seen that no actual rebuilding is taking place. The only Jews attempting to lay cornerstones are fringe groups who are sometimes labeled by fellow Israelis as extremists and "dangerous lunatics."[16] Sadly, some evangelical churches have collected donations for the rebuilding of the temple, channeling these funds to support such fringe groups.

But these Jewish sects are not the only extremists. Anticipating the rebuilding of the temple, some Christians hunt for ashes or embryos of red heifers! Red heifers, whose ashes are necessary for the purification of those who enter the temple to worship (Num 19:1-10), are currently sought in Europe for breeding in Israel. Some feel that the ashes of a living red heifer will suffice, while others—such as lay archaeologist Gary Collett—believe only the original red-heifer ashes will do.[17] So Collett has embarked on excavations to seek two-thousand-year-old red-heifer ashes.

If the temple is rebuilt, certain prophecy teachers claim, the antichrist will make a covenant of peace with Israel at the beginning of Daniel's seventieth week (the beginning of the so-called seven-year tribulation), and then three and a half years later he will violate the covenant by sitting in the temple and declaring himself to be God (Dan 9:27; compare 2 Thess 2:1-4).[18]

The rebuilding of the temple is being hindered by two problems: (1) disputes about the proper location for the temple and (2) conflicts with the Muslims.

1. There is no consensus regarding exactly where the temple is to be rebuilt. Some say that the Dome of the Rock or the Mosque of Omar lies directly over the original temple. Others, such as Shlomo Goren, former chief rabbi of Israel, claim the original temple was definitely west of the Dome of the Rock. Still others, such as Jewish physicist Ashur Kaufman, believe the temple is currently located under the Dome of the Spirits, northwest of the Dome of the Rock. But archaeologist Meir Ben-Dov claims the original temple is buried many feet underground, so no one can know with any certainty where the Holy of Holies originally stood.[19] In any case, mainline Jews have no interest in rebuilding a temple, for they believe that it will be rebuilt only after the Messiah arrives.[20]

2. The most popular site for the temple is owned by Muslims. The

Muslims possess the sanctuary known as the Dome of the Rock. They will not allow any Christian or Jew to openly pray on this site, and "the merest hint of rebuilding the Temple is considered an outrage by the Prophet's [Mohammed] followers, who in the words of an official at Al Aqsa, 'will defend the Islamic holy places to the last drop of their blood.' "[21] On three separate occasions one Jewish group attempted to lay a cornerstone at the entrance of the Temple Mount, only to be vehemently rebuked and pelted with rocks by Muslims. During one of these incidents Israeli police "raked the crowd with automatic weapons fire, leaving 125 wounded and 21 dead."[22]

Many temple hopefuls believe that a cataclysmic event, such as a war with Islam, or a Russian attack on Israel, or the rapture, or a great earthquake, must first take place. Once the Dome of the Rock has been destroyed or damaged, the Muslims will permit Israel to rebuild their temple on the site. The antichrist will then come into the picture, and temple sacrifices will be reinstated.

Let's assume a worst-case scenario. Suppose there is finally an agreement that the Dome of the Rock is the official temple site, a major earthquake occurs, the Dome of the Rock is damaged, and the temple is rebuilt. What necessitates that temple sacrifices not be reinstated until the antichrist is revealed? Even if we accept prophetic teachers' interpretation of Daniel 9:27, the antichrist will only cause the sacrifices to cease. We cannot conclude from this that he will be the one who causes them to *begin*. The antichrist's covenant may have nothing to do with temple sacrifices. So the Jews in Israel could reinstate sacrifices decades, perhaps even centuries or longer, before the antichrist makes a covenant with them.

Reason 42: We Do Not Know That Current Conflicts in the Middle East Will Lead to the Battle of Armageddon

"It's time to rejoice for the Christians. We're going home." So announced the late Charles Taylor, date-setter and host of the television show *Today in Bible Prophecy.* The occasion was the 1991 war in the Middle East. Taylor believed the war between Iraq and the U.S.-led coalition would lead to the end times and Armageddon (the final end-time battle described in Rev 16:12-21; 19:11-21). In fact, as evidenced by the increased sales in prophecy books that year, many agreed with Taylor.[23] The Reverend R. L. Hymers of the Fundamentalist Bible Tabernacle in Los Angeles said in a sermon that the Gulf crisis "may very well be . . . what unites the West under one man that the Bible calls the Antichrist."[24]

Why was Operation Desert Storm thought to be prophetically significant? It involved the United States and Middle East oil. It involved the United Nations and George Bush's pompous declarations about a New World Order. But now, looking back at the conflict, many are having second thoughts. Wars and conflicts abound in the Middle East. So far none have led to Armageddon. Sadly, little notice was ever taken of the hundreds of soldiers who accepted Christ as their Savior during the war.[25] That revival didn't fit with the bleak dooms-day picture drawn by date-setters.

Reason 43: We Do Not Know That the Current Peace in the Middle East Will Lead to the Battle of Armageddon

It caught us all by surprise. On September 13, 1993, Israeli prime minister Rabin and Palestinian Liberation Organization leader Yasser Arafat met in Washington, D.C., to sign a peace agreement as U.S. president Bill Clinton declared that hatred and suspicion, like the walls of Jericho, had fallen. Date-setters scratched their heads while fever-ishly contemplating how this event related to Bible prophecy. Some believe this event portends a Russian invasion of Israel. After all, it is when the Jews say, "Peace and safety," that sudden destruction will come upon them (1 Thess 5:3).

Notice the catch-22 surrounding war and peace. In times of peace, end-time soothsayers claim peace accords are a strategy employed by the antichrist. In times of conflict, they claim the sign of "wars and rumors of war" is being fulfilled.

The question on everybody's mind, naturally, was whether the 1993 peace accord would last. Hal Lindsey said that if the treaty held, Israel, having lost control of the Golan Heights and the Gaza Strip, would be defenseless in the face of an Arab attack. In such a position, the only way to retaliate would be by nuclear war. Hence if the peace treaty survived, Lindsey asserted, we would be very *very* close to the coming of Christ.[26] Televangelist Benny Hinn also believed the treaty indicated that the end was near. He assured the youths at his church that Christ would return before they would be able to purchase a cemetery plot.[27] Grant Jeffrey believed a Palestinian state would emerge within two to five years after the accord, and when the PLO grew stronger, it would attack Israel.[28]

Many Christians share this entirely jaundiced view of Arabs and the PLO, not objectively considering that perhaps both parties are simply tired of the bloodshed. If Arafat has a secret agenda, he is certainly paying a high price for it. Many Arabs feel he has signed his death warrant by negotiating with "the enemy." He may suffer the same fate as Egyptian president Anwar Sadat, who was assassinated after the Camp David agreement with Israel. On the same day of the 1993 peace accord, demonstrators in Lebanon shouted, "Death to Arafat!"[29]

The real question we should ask is not how long the peace accord will last, but whether the peace accord is a blessing from God. Palestinian Christians answer with an emphatic yes.

Western Christians have often overlooked the fact that among the Palestinian refugees are a number of Christians. In their zeal to defend Israel's "right" to the Holy Land, many American Christians neglect their Palestinian brothers and sisters, who number well over 100,000. Holy Land tour maps do not show Palestinian refugee camps as sites to be visited. It would not be good for business if Western Christians were to see Christians in Palestine who suffer poverty and injustice.

Israel is not exempt from the need to recognize the human rights of others. We have every right to criticize inhumane Israeli activities, especially when they violate the rights of Palestinian Christians. It is the latter group who are presently the heirs of God's eternal promises.

We need not speculate about how long the peace accord will last. Instead, we should do what is biblical—pray for the peace of Jerusalem (Ps 122:6-7).

Reason 44: We Do Not Know That the Former Soviet Union Is Gog and Magog

"Biblical scholars have been saying for generations that Gog must be Russia. What other powerful nation is to the north of Israel? None," declared Ronald Reagan at a dinner speech in California in 1971.[30] Later, during Reagan's U.S. presidency, the nuclear arms race escalated because the "evil empire" was believed to pose a major threat to national security. In 1984 "one hundred prominent religious leaders urged Reagan to disavow the dogma that nuclear holocaust is foreordained in the Bible."[31]

Russia is often named as the prophetic Gog and Magog that will attack Israel and be destroyed by God (Ezek 38—39). Although the Bible never actually says this end-time enemy is Russia, dogmatism runs rampant. Provoking titles such as *The Coming Russian Invasion of Israel,* by Thomas S. McCall and Zola Levitt, and *Russia Will Attack Israel,* by Ray Comfort, make the speculation seem like indisputable fact. Author Tim LaHaye writes, "Russia is unquestionably the nation identified in the prophecies of Ezekiel 38 and 39."[32] William Goetz, author of the bestseller *Apocalypse Next,* claims that Russia's attack on Israel "is not a question of *if,* but *when.*"[33] Some have even ventured to establish exactly "when" this will all take place. David Webber of Southwest Radio Church and author C. S. Lovett both suggested that the invasion would occur in 1983.[34] Jack Van Impe suggested a date of 1999.[35]

Even after the communist Soviet Union disbanded, the prophetic dogmatism did not. Instead of reevaluating their prophecy interpretations, many speculators now question the motives of the leaders of the former Soviet Union. Their distrust didn't begin with Russia's turn to democracy, but back in the late 1980s when Mikhail Gorbachev promoted *glasnost*. Southwest Radio Church warned that the new openness "is really a façade meant to deceive the West."[36] James McKeever, editor of *End Times News Digest,* claimed *glasnost* was "a KGB-inspired campaign to soften Western resolve against Communism."[37] If this were true, the plan backfired. *Glasnost* eventually opened the way for a possible Russian democracy. Though that country's current political situation remains unstable, Russia is now experiencing spiritual revival and new freedom. Nevertheless, the speculators relentlessly condemn it as God's enemy—Gog and Magog. A lack of food will now apparently lead Boris Yeltsin to attack Israel, asserts prophetic teacher Hilton Sutton.[38]

But Russia wasn't always the bad guy. During the Middle Ages, the Turkish Ottoman Empire was thought to be Ezekiel's Gog and Magog. During the pioneer days of America, Puritan writer Cotton Mather believed Gog and Magog were the American Indians![38] The Muslims will probably be next.

What is the true identity of Gog and Magog and their cohorts? Let's first examine why Russia is *not* Gog and Magog, and then I will offer an interpretation that identifies Gog and Magog. First, Rosh does not mean Russia. Ezekiel 38:2 names the main minions of Gog and Magog as Rosh, Meshech and Tubal. Contrary to prophecy buffs, Rosh is not an older form of the word *Russia*. Rather, the term stands for "chief" or "prince" in Hebrew. *Russia* is derived from the term *Rus,* a word originating with the Middle Age Vikings from the northern Black Sea. It originally meant "seafarers" or "rowing."

Second, Meshech and Tubal are not Russian cities. They are often falsely identified with the Russian cities Moscow and Tobolsk. Ancient sources clearly attest, through Josephus, Herodotus and cuneiform inscriptions, that these names are associated with Mushku and Tabal in Anatolia, the Asiatic region of Turkey.[39]

Third, Gomer and Togarmah are not Eastern European nations. Other invaders who will accompany Gog are Gomer and Togarmah (Ezek 38:6). These were said to be East Germany and the other Eastern Bloc nations. Now that communism has collapsed in Eastern Europe, little mention is made of the two! Actually, Gomer and Togarmah trace back to the Cimmerians, a group that originally lived near the Black Sea but apparently died out in the area of Hungary by 500 B.C.[40]

What about Persia, Cush and Put, which some interpret as Iran, Ethiopia and Libya? These names are best understood as symbolic for nations from the far ends of the earth. We will see why in a few more paragraphs.

The fact that Gog and Magog are north of Israel does not indicate they are coming from Russia. Geographically, the hordes of Gog would come from the north because this was the way most of Israel's enemies invaded—through the Fertile Crescent along the Euphrates River.[41] The Babylonians, for instance, were a northern threat from "a distant land" (Is 39:3; Jer 5:15; 6:22; 50:41). Josephus called Gog and Magog the Scythians (*Antiquities* 1.6.1). This group was later understood as the Goths, who sacked Rome in A.D. 410.[42] The Goths then migrated west and were destroyed in Italy and Spain. *Therefore, no modern nation has ancestors directly traceable to the original Gog and Magog.*

Furthermore, we run into major difficulties if we interpret Gog and Magog's attack in a strict, literal manner. Do we honestly think Russia would invade Israel with horses, spears, and wooden bows and arrows (Ezek 38:15; 39:3, 9-10, 20)? Some have convoluted the issue by claiming the Russians have made new weapons out of a wooden product called lignostone to evade radar detection. Even if this were true, it still doesn't explain away the horses or the spears, war clubs, and bows and arrows that will be used for fuel for several years.[43] Will the arrows be nuclear-tipped? Bomb-tipped arrows popularized on the silver screen are still no match for Israel's automatic weaponry, tanks and aircraft—unless, of course, every Russian fights like Rambo! It is simply ludicrous to think that Russian generals would have their forces battle with ancient weapons.

Revelation 20: The Key to Gog's Identity. It is best to understand Gog and Magog as symbolic for the heathen from the four quarters of the earth who will attack God's people at the end of the millennium. This makes sense when we realize that the prophetic doom of the rest of Israel's enemies is described in Ezekiel 25—32. The hordes of Gog and Magog become the last enemies of God's people.

If you read Ezekiel 32:21 to 39:29 in one sitting, it becomes evident that these chapters can be fulfilled only during the thousand-year reign of Christ, the millennium (see Rev 20). Israel is depicted as regenerated (Ezek 36), and the Messiah (Jesus Christ)—symbolically portrayed as King David—reigns over them (Ezek 37:24-28). The people of God dwell safely in unwalled cities because Christ has made a true covenant of peace with them (Ezek 38:7-8, 11, 14; compare 39:26). All this will take place in the latter end of history (Ezek 38:8).

Although Ezekiel's account is more detailed, both Ezekiel 38—39 and Revelation 20:7-10 clearly depict the same final attack, with Gog and Magog as the last enemy of God's people. Revelation 20 places this final invasion at the end of the millennium. If we interpret the millennium as a literal thousand years, as most speculators do, we must assume that Gog and Magog will not attack Israel until one thousand years after Christ has overthrown the current world system—Russia, Germany, Iran, Ethiopia and Libya included.

Finally, Gog attacks God's "people Israel"—"the camp of God's people" (Ezek 38:16; Rev 20:9). These titles could hardly be applied to the nation of Israel before the millennium. Prior to the Second Coming, Jerusalem seems to be the "Sodom and Egypt" of Revelation 11:8. Prophetic speculators have yet to come up with one solid reason why Ezekiel 38—39 and Revelation 20 do not refer to the same Gog and Magog. Since Ezekiel 38—39 speaks of the millennium, neither Russia nor any other current nation can be called the prophetic Gog and Magog.

Reason 45: We Do Not Know That the European Community Is the Revived Roman Empire

As I sit at my computer writing this book, today's headlines blare out: "What Arms Talks Were in Cold War, Trade Talks Are Now." In Geneva, the United States has reached a trading accord with the European Community (EC) under the General Agreement on Tariffs and Trade (GATT). The agreement's target date for going into effect is July 1, 1995.[44] Doubtless, some speculator will exploit this date as the beginning of the Great Tribulation because the EC is considered the Revived Roman Empire, a confederacy of ten nations out of which will arise the antichrist (Dan 2:39-45; 7:7-14; Rev 13; 17). Noah Hutchings of Southwest Radio Church calls it "the Federated Roman Empire that will produce the Antichrist and the False Prophet."[45] Jack Van Impe declared that when the EC came to power on January 1, 1993, the countdown to Armageddon would begin.[46] In his 1970 book *I Predict,* Salem Kirban wrote: "Within the next 20 years I predict the United States will merge with European nations under one dictatorial-type leader."[47]

But unlike the ten nations represented as ten horns in Revelation 13:1, the EC currently has twelve members (unless one includes all the nations involved in GATT, which are 117!). To account for this discrepancy, prophecy teachers speculate that the number of nations will fluctuate, but the final number will settle at ten.

Yet there is also no agreement that these ten nations are the EC. Tim LaHaye believes the ten horns refer to ten global regions,[48] while others claims the ten nations are from Islam.[49] Many scholars, on the other hand, affirm that the seven heads symbolize completeness, while the ten horns allude to Daniel's beast (Dan 7:7, 24) and symbolically represent Satan's might.[50] Thus, the prophetic image "is a picture of the fullness of evil in all its hideous strength."[51]

A further consideration: this is not the first time since the fall of the Roman Empire that a European community of nations has revived. In A.D. 800, during the papacy of Pope Leo III, King Charlemagne of the Franks became the first king of the Holy Roman Empire. This kingdom, also known as the First Reich (empire), prevailed until the Napoleonic Wars of 1806. A Christian living in medieval times had the same reasons as we do to believe the final kingdom had arrived. One Holy Roman emperor named Frederick II (reigning 1215-1250), who as a child had been raised under the supervision of Pope Innocent III, rebelled against the pontiff, opposing and exalting himself above the church. Even the papacy, which was itself quite secularized at this time, thought Frederick was the antichrist.[52] But after many hundreds of years, the Holy Roman Empire faded into the annals of history. We should be willing to admit that the European Community might also one day disband without producing the antichrist.

When *should* we be concerned about the European Community? We should become concerned if out of ten nations there arises one definite leader who ends up sitting in the temple of God and claims that he alone is God (2 Thess 2:1-4). Until then, let the EC trade in peace.

Samuel Bacchiocchi, a contributing writer for *End-Times News Digest,* writes:

It is unimaginable for anyone familiar with the political fragmentation existing in most of the ten nations belonging to the European Common Market that a political dictator could ever succeed today in dominating all these ten nations without a bloody resistance. In my own country of Italy, for example, where we have more than a dozen political parties and where coalition governments have fallen dozens of times since 1945, it is inconceivable that all political parties would suddenly support a European political-religious dictator. If nations such as England, France, Belgium, Holland, and Poland fought heroically against Hitler's attempt to dominate them, there is every reason to believe that they are prepared to fight again even more heroically today against anyone making a similar attempt to control them.[53]

Reason 46: We Do Not Know That the United States Is the Whore of Babylon

The End-Time Handmaidens relate a vision of A. A. Allen, a popular faith healer who died of sclerosis of the liver due to alcoholism. When Allen was at the top of the Empire State Building, he saw the Statue of Liberty stagger and fall like a drunk. A black cloud then engulfed her, and "Liberty began to cough." Then "the statue was in agony; she fell to her knees and finally fell dead into the Gulf."[54]

The United States will soon suffer doomsday, according to certain speculators, because it is the whore of Babylon prophesied in Revelation 17—18. Prophecy author James Lloyd claims, "*Babylon* is in the United States of America. She is *New York City,* and she is scheduled for utter destruction in the near future. . . . People are usually surprised to see the similarities between the woman representing Babylon in Revelation [17:3-5], and the woman that is The Statue of Liberty."[55] Mary Stewart Relfe claimed that "America will burn," being totally destroyed sometime around 1993-1994, about three years before the Battle of Armageddon in 1997.[56]

Similarities between America and the whore of Babylon relate to the luxurious materialism that marks the description of Babylon in Revelation 17 and 18. Any wealthy nation, of course, is suspect. James McKeever, for instance, believes Babylon could represent the Arab OPEC nations with their vast oil reserves.[57]

If the United States is Babylon, where are all the Christians it has martyred (Rev 17:6; 18:20, 24)? Also, since America now condemns slavery, how is it that the nation will revert to the slave trade mentioned in Revelation 18:12-13? Indeed America—epitomized by New York—is sinful and corrupt, but it currently fails to meet all the qualifications for the whore of Babylon.

Reason 47: We Do Not Know That the Roman Catholic Church Is the Whore of Babylon

Another candidate for the whore of Babylon is the Roman Catholic

Church. Bestselling author Dave Hunt writes, "That this 'last days' Babylon is described as a *woman* again identifies her as the Roman Catholic Church, for who a *woman*—'the Virgin Mary'—is the dominant deity."[58] Some Protestants trace Catholic practices back to the Babylonian religion, with its reported mother and child idols said to be the forerunners of Virgin Mary statues. Catholicism turned pagan, they claim, as soon as Constantine became emperor in the fourth century.

This fundamentalist teaching demonstrates the amazing ignorance certain Protestants have of church history. The Catholic Church and the Eastern Orthodox Church were *the* Christian church of the Middle Ages. Regardless of their errors and faulty teachings, they are living proof that Christ has kept his promise to preserve his church throughout all ages (Mt 16:16-18; Lk 1:33; Eph 3:21; Jude 3).[59] Moreover, the church did not become apostate after Constantine became emperor. If this was the case, we should throw away our current New Testament and the Nicene and Chalcedon creeds, because the canon of our twenty-seven New Testament books, though always inspired, was first ratified during this time, along with the orthodox creeds of the church.

Three objections usually arise at this point. (1) Doesn't Rome have seven hills as described in Revelation 17:6-9? (2) Didn't Rome murder many saints during the Spanish Inquisition and other persecutions (Rev 17:6; 18:24)? (3) Isn't Mary-worship connected with Babylonian paganism? Let's address these questions.

1. Hills or kingdoms? The Greek word rendered "hills" *(orē)* in Revelation 17:9 can be rendered "mountains" (compare KJV) and may figuratively represent world powers (Jer 51:25; Dan 2:35; Zech 4:7) instead of the topography of Rome. It is the whore of Babylon that is the city (Rev 17:18), not the scarlet beast with the seven heads representing seven mountains (Rev 17:9-10). Thus it seems unlikely that the beast is symbolic of the city of Rome.[60] In keeping with John's symbolic use of the number 7, the seven-headed beast represents the completeness of Satanic wickedness.

It is true that according to ancient geography, Rome proverbially rested on seven hills. But this does not mean that the end-time kingdom *must* be Rome, let alone the Catholic Church. If there is any allusion to Rome in this passage, all this prophecy would convey is that the final Satanic system will share certain characteristics with the Roman Empire. Such characteristics would include emperor worship and persecution of the church (compare Rev 13:1-7). There is no evidence, however, that the system itself is geographically located where the old city of Rome stood.

2. *Who's persecuting whom?* It's true that Roman Catholicism has been guilty of persecutions. Yet not only did Catholics persecute Protestants, but Protestants also persecuted Catholics. If Catholics are guilty of shedding innocent blood, so are Protestants. Millions of soldiers from both Catholic and Protestant faiths died fighting against each other in religious wars (such as the Thirty Years' War, 1618-1648). And both churches persecuted Anabaptists and heretics.

Even to stop with these facts, however, would be to overlook an important historical consideration and to fail to identify the ultimate persecutor. As medieval Europe became fragmented, kings and bishops often worked hand in hand, and ambitious kings frequently took over the local church in an effort to unify their realms. A historian taking this into account shows us the real culprits behind the Spanish Inquisition:

> Spain had long been remarkable among European lands as a place where three religions—Islam, Judaism, and Christianity—coexisted with a certain degree of toleration. This toleration was to end dramatically under [King] Ferdinand and [Queen] Isabella, who made Spain the prime example of state-controlled religion. Ferdinand and Isabella exercised almost total control over the Spanish church as they placed religion in the service of national unity. They appointed the higher clergy and the officers of the Inquisition.[61]

Revelation 17—18 similarly draws a picture of a demonically controlled state, not a religious body, that is the ultimate persecutor of the saints. This is in keeping with both Old and New Testament histories. It is probably better to view the persecutor in Revelation 17—18 as a conglomeration of all world powers that have persecuted God's people. Empires such as Egypt, Assyria, Babylon and Rome have opposed both God and God's people. This is also consistent with the image in King Nebuchadnezzar's dream (Dan 2). The image is a conglomeration of kingdoms (Babylon, Medo-Persia, Greece and Rome, which might prefigure the final empire in the last days that will oppose God), not just one.

3. Idolatry of religion or materialism? The Roman Catholic veneration of Mary has nothing to do with an idolatrous Babylonian prototype of Madonna and baby Jesus images (even though such Catholic images sometimes do lead practitioners into idolatry). For one thing, there are not two separate Babylons in Revelation 17—18. The connections between these two chapters are much too similar to dichotomize them between a religious and a commercial Babylon (Rev 17:3-5, 18; 18:15-17). The whore of Babylon is a political city that makes idolatrous claims. In Revelation 17—18 its religious crimes are persecuting the saints and casting spells on merchants (Rev 17:6; 18:23).[62] The whore has led millions into the idolatry of materialism, not graven images.

Is there any connection between Babylon and Rome? Bruce Metzger writes: "Just as Babylon represented to the Hebrews all that was wicked and symbolized persecution, so for John [the author of Revelation], Rome was another Babylon, the source and fountainhead of all seductive luxury and vice, living in voluptuous materialism and selfishness."[63] The best way to interpret the whore of Babylon, however, is to see her as an archetype alluding to all the previous God-dishonoring empires and systems—from the Tower of Babel to communism—and pointing to the final end-times system that will oppose God. There is simply no sufficient reason to dogmatically claim this final system is the Roman Catholic Church.

Reason 48: We Do Not Know That Iraq Will Succeed in Rebuilding Babylon to Its Former Glory

The poster read:

FROM NEBUCHADNEZZAR TO SADDAM HUSSEIN
BABYLON UNDERGOES A RENAISSANCE.

Portraying profiles of Saddam and Nebuchadnezzar side by side, it marked the Babylonian International Festival held September 22 to October 22, 1987. The strongman of Iraq has stated his wish to restore ancient Babylon to the glory it enjoyed during the sixth century B.C., when Nebuchadnezzar destroyed Jerusalem.

Capitalizing on Saddam's vision, Charles Dyer wrote *The Rise Of Babylon: Sign of the End Times,* which sold 300,000 copies during the Persian Gulf War. The front of his book says, "Startling photos from Iraq reveal that SADDAM HUSSEIN is rebuilding the lost city of Babylon. The Bible says Babylon will be rebuilt in the last days. *Could ours be the last generation?"*[64] And the back cover warns, "Saddam Hussein is rebuilding Babylon to the exact specifications and splendor it had in the days of Nebuchadnezzar."

A Western diplomat observing the reconstruction claimed, however, that this new "splendor" pales in comparison to that ancient Babylon: "What they are doing is pretty tacky. . . . They are putting up all this cheap new brick work on top of the old walls, and it looks quite awful."[65] If Saddam could not even take Kuwait, what makes us think he will restore Babylon to become a major world power? At the present time Iraq does not have the power or the commercial potential to become the wealthy and influential Babylon depicted in the end-times prophecies of Scripture.

In any case, Revelation 17—18 does not indicate that Babylon will be literally restored to its previous splendor. Rather, Babylon here most likely represents all the kingdoms who blaspheme God and oppose his people.

Remember, most prophetic writings in Scripture are highly symbolic. When we read Revelation too literally, we miss its meaning.

Reason 49: We Do Not Know That Current Ecumenical Movements and Alliances Are Part of the Antichrist's Final Kingdom

"Is Chuck Colson, then, a wolf in sheep's clothing—a born again New Ager *disguised* as an evangelical Christian?" asks Texe Marrs, bestselling author of books such as *Dark Secrets of the New Age* and *Mystery Mark of the New Age*. Colson, Marrs writes, as the head of the "money-hungry" Prison Fellowship, may have "sold his soul to the Devil" by accepting the Templeton Prize at the Parliament of World Religions in Chicago, held August 28 to September 4, 1993.[66] Why such strong accusations? According to certain scaremongers, the Parliament launched the New Age Aquarian "Plan" for a single world government by the year 2000.[67]

To these sensationalists' chagrin, Colson preached an uncompromised Christianity at his acceptance speech, mentioning Christ as the way, the truth and the life (John 14:6) and stating that humankind is sinful and depraved. He also asserted that the New World Order is one of the "political illusions" of our day and proclaimed that God sent his "only Son to die on a the cross that our sins might be forgiven, and that we might live free. . . . By the cross he offers hope. By the resurrection he assures his triumph. Make no mistake, this cannot be delayed, or resisted. Mankind's only choice is to recognize him now or in the moment of ultimate judgment."[68]

The Parliament of World Religions, the World Council of Churches, the United Nations and other ecumenical alliances—whether religious or secular—are favorite targets for end-times speculators. No doubt the Parliament of World Religions attempted to exalt religious harmony and global unity couched in New Age terms, but was the New Age "Plan" successfully launched at this event? One small Hindu group heckled a couple of speakers. Greek Orthodox representatives pulled out, appalled at the many "quasi-religious groups" represented at the Parliament. Four Jewish groups walked out, angered that Louis Farrakhan of the Nation of Islam was one of the speakers.[69]

Not quite a successful New Age conspiracy!

The United Nations may not be the end-time system any more than were the now-almost-forgotten League of Nations and Concert of Europe. And is there any definitive proof that the World Council of Churches is unifying all religions when it still does not admit Jehovah's Witnesses, Mormons and many other cults? Even if one of these alliances were the forerunner of the final end-times system, the existence of such alliances does not indicate how close we are to the end. The only thing that has happened so far is that prophetic pundits have slandered Christians like Chuck Colson.

Reason 50: We Do Not Know That the New World Order Is the Final End-Time System

George Bush described the New World Order as "a world quite different from the one we've known. A world where the rule of law supplants the rule of the jungle. A world in which the nations recognize and share responsibility for freedom and justice. A world where the strong respect the rights of the weak."[70] The phrase "New World Order" reportedly was coined by former Soviet leader Mikhail Gorbachev, who spoke before the United Nations of a need for a New World Order on December 7, 1988.[71]

Since then a number of prophecy books—such as the bestseller written by former presidential candidate Pat Robertson, entitled *The New World Order,* Donald S. McAlvany's *Toward A New World Order: The Countdown to Armageddon* and Gary Kah's *En Route to Global Occupation*—have rehashed the phrase. Most prophecy books on the New World Order define it as the end-times system characterized by global peace, Freemason conspiracy links and New Age agendas. Pastor Clyde Edminster of Woodbrook Chapel, Rainier, Washington, taught that between 1993 and 1996, the antichrist would reign over the world through the New World Order.[72]

Prophecy hypes even tell us we can see this end-time system on the back of any one-dollar bill (see figure 2). The Great Seal of the United

Figure 2. The Great Seal of the United States.

States shows a pyramid topped by an eye; the Latin phrase *NOVUS ORDO SECLORUM,* which means "new world order," rests at the pyramid's foot. Irrefutable proof? Not quite. The symbols appear Masonic, but this doesn't mean they trace back to any conspiracy. The all-seeing eye is that of the Grand Architect, the Masons' title for God. The Latin words overarching the pyramid, *ANNUIT CŒPTIS,* mean "he has favored our undertakings." The pyramid alludes to the Jews' being freed from Egyptian slavery and thus symbolizes God's providence over America, and perhaps freedom from the oppression of Great Britain.

It is easy to see how the founding fathers of America (many of whom were apparently both Christians and Masons) would combine Masonic and biblical terms and imagery to symbolize their new freedom. The early American settlers often called the Americas "the New World." Since they had withstood Great Britain in the Revolutionary War, "New World Order" in this context is nothing more than a reference to the establishment of the republic of the United States in 1776.

Some new world orders date back even further than this. Prophecies of a new world order in 1186 were circulated in a document by astrologers, called the "Letter of Toledo," during the Third Crusade.[73] In the seventeenth century England spoke of a "new order" after the defeat and beheading of Charles I in 1649.[74] More recently, Hitler also promoted a new world order, anticipating a thousand-year Reich.[75]

What can we learn from this? First, we should admit the phrase "new world order" is hundreds of years old. As the examples above demonstrate, the only things that are really new about the New World Order are the meanings poured into the term.

Second, there is no sufficient evidence that a New Age or Illuminati conspiracy is calling the shots for the New World Order so that even leaders like Gorbachev and Bush are its pawns. Politicians, in their bipartisan maneuvers, are notorious for making promises and hyperbolic statements, using flowery terminology and supporting certain clubs or societies without fully realizing the impact and ramifications of their actions. Politicians may be guilty of thinking they can solve all the world's problems, but this is not enough to make them guilty of a global conspiracy.

Third, even if a certain person, group or nation deliberately attempted to fulfill the role of the Beast or Babylon in Revelation, they would not necessarily succeed in doing so. If Mikhail Gorbachev, Bill Clinton, Ross Perot, Saddam Hussein or Al Gore claimed to be the antichrist, this would not make him the antichrist any more than Sun Myung Moon's claim to be Christ makes him Christ. No human will ultimately determine who is the antichrist—only God will. No human will ultimately determine the nations of the antichrist's kingdom— only God will. No human will determine prophetic dates for the future—only God will.

8
Reasons Why No One Knows the Date Through Modern-Day "Prophets"

*A*s members of the Great White Brotherhood fell down and kissed the feet of their white-robed messiah, Maria Devi Khrystos, she cried out that the world would end November 24, 1993. Her followers could not doubt her, for she was the "living god" and "eternal prophet." But as the predicted doomsday approached, "god" (Khrystos) changed her mind. She moved the new Judgment Day to November 14, when, after committing suicide, she would rise from the dead in three days. Her husband Yuri Kryvonohov, alias John Swami, founder of the cult, had originally declared himself to be God but had passed this honor to his wife in 1990. Fearing mass suicide among the members (who reportedly number 150,000), Ukrainian authorities jailed six hundred of the devotees and their two leaders.[1] Nothing unusual transpired on November 14, 1993.

The Great White Brotherhood is one of many cults that have flourished in the former Soviet Union ever since the collapse of communism. Accounts like this one compel us to realize how self-proclaimed prophets still wield influence over the masses. After the cult tragedies in Jonestown, Guyana (1978), and Waco, Texas (1993), we might think that no one would follow another Jim Jones or David Koresh. Tragically, this is not the case. False teachers and false messiahs abound, and like their Christian counterparts, they too proclaim the end is near. But when their predicted doomsday tarries, it only confirms that they are indeed false prophets.

Reason 51: Visions, Dreams and Trances Cannot Give Us Correct End-Time Dates

When Edgar Cayce was about seven years old, a figure who was as bright as the sun called him to his psychic vocation. From then on, Cayce, who came to be known as the "sleeping prophet," would fall into trances diagnosing illnesses and receiving visions of the future. He reportedly predicted the stock-market crash in 1929 and the end of the Great Depression in 1933.[2] Since those early days, Edgar Cayce has become a household name, and his prophecies are studied to this day at the Association for Research and Enlightenment: Reincarnation and Karma centers throughout America.

Cayce also predicted massive changes on the earth from 1958 to 1998. New York would be destroyed and San Francisco and Los Angeles would slip into the Pacific Ocean, while the lost continent of Atlantis would resurface from the Atlantic Ocean. This cataclysmic era "will be proclaimed as the periods when His Light will be seen again in the clouds."[3]

Are such visions reliable? Cayce envisioned that a prominent land, like the original Atlantis, would be destroyed around 1976. And China was to gravitate toward Christianity in 1968.[4] Both these dates failed, and as 1998 approaches it looks as though Cayce's other prophecies will also prove false.[5] It is evident that Edgar Cayce, who also believed

Jesus Christ was a reincarnated being, did not receive his prophecies from God.

You may say to yourselves, "How can we know when a message has not been spoken by the LORD?" If what a prophet proclaims in the name of the LORD does not take place or come true, that is a message the LORD has not spoken. That prophet has spoken presumptuously. Do not be afraid of him. (Deut 18:21-22)

Yet today even certain evangelicals claim to receive similar prophetic visions. Mary Stewart Relfe declared, "*The WORD OF THE LORD CAME to me:* 'COUNTDOWN TO THE GREAT TRIBULATION. ... MAKE A CHART WITH A COLUMN FOR THE YEARS 1983 TO 1990.' "[6] Relfe concluded that the Great Tribulation would begin in 1990, with Babylon's (America's) destruction in 1993 and Christ's kingdom established on earth in 1998.[7]

When anyone claims to have received a vision concerning the end of the world, beware of dates attached to it. The Lord will give no revelation beyond what he has given regarding the time of his return (Mt 24:36; Acts 1:7).[8]

Reason 52: The Predictions of Modern-Day "Prophets" Are Not 100 Percent Accurate

Some say he's Elijah, others say he's the Son of Man. Many claim he was virgin-born, and certain followers pray to him and baptize in his name. With 300,000 followers worldwide, the legend of William Branham lives on.[9] Followers insist he was always correct in his revelations and healed everyone he laid hands on. He claimed to receive his power from an angel—a well-built man with long dark hair—who would operate through Branham when he was in a trancelike state.[10]

His calling was dramatic. On the day of his birth, a bright light supposedly shone upon him. When he came to adulthood, a voice from heaven reportedly told him, "As John the Baptist was sent to forerun the first coming of Jesus Christ, so are you sent to forerun His Second Coming."[11] One of Branham's most popular portraits shows what appears to be a halo over his head. During the 1950s his popularity as a faith healer was second only to that of Oral Roberts.

On February 28, 1963, two years before his death, the seven angels of the book of Revelation allegedly appeared to Branham and two other witnesses, fulfilling the "sign of the Son of Man" in Matthew 24:30. On that date a mysterious cloud ring appeared in the sky over Flagstaff, Arizona, about twenty-six miles high and thirty miles wide. This sign reportedly marked the end of the Laodicean age (Rev 3:20) and the beginning of the Bride age, in which Christ is calling his church out of the creeds of orthodox Christianity.[12] In Branham's view, all the various church denominations are the antichrist, and both Catholics and Protestants are spiritual harlots.[13]

Popular charismatics such as Oral Roberts, Benny Hinn, Kenneth Hagin and Paul Cain believe Branham was a great man of God, if not a prophet. Branham was not the first holiness preacher so designated. Dynamic speakers and faith healers are often heralded on Christian networks as anointed prophets of God. In the late nineteenth century, John Alexander Dowie and Charles Parham, leading influences on the Pentecostal movement, were both considered by some to be Elijah.[14]

Was William Branham a true prophet of God? Let's look at his prophecies. He predicted the millennium would begin in 1977.[15] Moreover, under the supposed influence of the Holy Spirit Branham claimed: "Trinitarianism is of the Devil, I say that thus Saith the Lord! . . . And as far as three Gods, that's from hell."[16] If we accept this "revelation" at face value, not only does God reject the Trinity, but he doesn't even comprehend it! Trinitarians do not believe in three gods but confess one God who is three Persons—the Father, Son and Holy Spirit (see Mt 28:19; Acts 5:3-4; Gal 1:3; Heb 1:8). Furthermore, wherever Branham's predictions were inaccurate, he was not hearing from God, according to the Bible's criterion (Deut 18:20-22).

Although Branham apparently did perform many miracles, he taught false doctrine and denied the Trinity. The Bible tells us:

If a prophet, or one who foretells by dreams, appears among you and announces to you a miraculous sign or wonder, and if the sign or wonder of which he has spoken takes place, and he says, "Let us follow other gods" (gods you have not known) "and let us worship them," you must not listen to the words of that prophet or dreamer. The LORD your God is testing you to find out whether you love him with all your heart and with all your soul. It is the LORD your God you must follow, and him you must revere. (Deut 13:1-4)

Reason 53: Many Modern "Prophets" Teach False Doctrine

In 1959 the Reverend Jim Jones had a vision that Indianapolis would be destroyed in a great holocaust.[17] This prophecy never came to pass. But Jones eventually claimed to be Christ in human flesh. After the failures of his specific predictions, his followers should have known better than to follow him to Guyana, where on November 18, 1978, Jones led them in a mass suicide that claimed the lives of over nine hundred men, women and children. If they had studied and heeded the Word of God, they would have known he was a false prophet.

Moses David Berg, leader of the Children of God, proclaimed that a comet called Kohoutek would destroy America, the whore of Babylon, in 1973. When that prophecy failed, members should have left the self-proclaimed prophet. Instead many remained faithful to him, and some women from the cult became "hookers for Jesus" to win lost souls to their sect. Berg also predicted that the tribulation would begin in 1989, with Christ's return in 1993.[18] Now called the Family, Berg's group is desperately attempting to shed their former image despite the child abuse and prostitution charges they face in France, Argentina and Paraguay.[19] Their recent tract "The Endtime News!" speaks of the return of Christ within "THE NEXT FEW YEARS!"

Then there's the Church Universal and Triumphant, headed by Elizabeth Clare Prophet, who allegedly receives her messages from the "Ascended Masters"—spiritual beings who guide humankind in their evolution process. Prophet, also known as Guru Ma, received a message from Ascended Master El Morya that the United States might go to war with the Soviet Union on October 2, 1989. The date then changed to December 31 and finally to April 23, 1990. To prepare for the coming Armageddon, members of the Church Universal and Triumphant moved to Paradise, Montana, and "have constructed massive fallout shelters stockpiled with food, medical supplies, diesel generators, and computers."20

Members should have known that these prophets were false not only because they predicted false dates (Deut 18:21-22) but also because Jesus says we can know false prophets by the fruit of their teaching and conduct (Mt 7:15-21). These self-appointed messiahs, psychics and sexual abusers bear the fruit of false doctrine and sinfulness. By consulting the Ascended Masters, for example, Guru Ma is directly violating the doctrine of Christ as our only mediator (Mt 11:27; Jn 14:6; 1 Tim 2:5). The apostle Paul fervently warns that such false teachers are preaching a counterfeit Christ and a counterfeit gospel through a counterfeit spirit (2 Cor 11:1-15; compare Gal 1:8-9; 1 Jn 4:1-6).

Reason 54: Jehovah's Witnesses Are False Prophets

Pat was a Jehovah's Witness I invited to my apartment a number of years ago. She brought with her an elder, a man who had been a diligent Watchtower student for many years. I asked them about the false prophecies the Watchtower had made. The gentleman admitted that his organization had made mistakes. I pressed him to acknowledge that false prophecy is more than a mere "mistake." No renunciation of the Watchtower occurred that morning, but the two "Bible students" left with puzzled looks on their faces.

False prophecies have embellished Watchtower literature ever since their founder, Charles Taze Russell, taught that Christ returned in October 1874. One hundred years later (1974), Jehovah's Witnesses were commended because "reports are heard of brothers selling their homes and property and planning to finish out the rest of their days in this old system in the pioneer service. Certainly this is a fine way to spend the short time remaining before the wicked world's end."[21] The Watchtower—which claims to be God's prophet for this era[22]— declared the end would take place in 1975.

Below is a list of some of the Jehovah's Witnesses' most remarkable blunders.

Date	Prophecy	Source
1874	"Our Lord, the appointed King, is now present, since October 1874."	*The Battle of Armageddon,* vol. 4 of *Studies in the Scriptures* (1914 ed.), p. 621
1914	"The 'battle of the great day of God Almighty' . . . will end in A.D. 1914."	*The Time Is at Hand,* vol. 2 of *Studies in the Scriptures* (1908 ed.), p. 101
1925	"Therefore we may confidently expect that 1925 will mark the return of Abraham, Isaac, Jacob and the faithful prophets of old."	*Millions Now Living Will Never Die* (1920), p. 89
1941	"The Lord's provided instrument for most effective work in the remaining months before Armageddon."	*The Watchtower,* September 15, 1941, p. 288
1942	"We may expect to see Daniel and the other mentioned princes any day now!"	*Consolation,* May 27, 1942, p. 13
1975	"1975 will mark the end of 6,000 years of human history since Adam's creation."	*The Watchtower,* August 15, 1968, p. 494

Reason 55: The Mormons' Founder, Joseph Smith, Was a False Prophet

The Mormons are another sect with a long track record of false prophecies. In 1832 founder Joseph Smith Jr. prophesied under "divine revelation" of Christ "the gathering of his saints to stand upon Mount Zion, which shall be the city of New Jerusalem. Which city shall be built, beginning at the temple lot, which is appointed by the finger of the Lord, in the western boundaries of the State of Missouri. . . . Which temple shall be reared in this generation." Moreover, "Zion shall not be moved out of her place. . . . And, behold, there is none other place appointed than that which I have appointed; neither shall there be any other place appointed."[23]

Like many of today's evangelicals, Smith believed he was living in the final generation: "Pestilence, hail, famine and earthquake will sweep the wicked of this generation from off the face of the land, to open and prepare the way for the return of the lost tribes of Israel from the north country. . . . There are those now living upon the earth whose eyes shall not be closed in death until they see all these things, which I have spoken, fulfilled."[24] But the generation living in 1832 passed away with no Missouri temple. Contrary to Smith's prophecy, another temple *was* appointed—his successor Brigham Young led the new sect to its current temple site in Salt Lake City, Utah.

After Joseph Smith's death, the "prophets" of the Latter Day Saints have continued in the tradition of false prophecies and doctrines. In spite of these errors, the Mormon church keeps growing. Instead of listening to their faulty prophets, Mormons should examine the Bible, which clearly warns us to stay away from false teachers and prophets (Deut 18:20-21; Jer 14:13-15; 23:15-40; 27:14-15; 28:8-9; Ezek 14:10; Mt 7:15).

Reason 56: Jeane Dixon Is a False Prophet

False prophets come in all shapes, sizes and sexes. Jeane Dixon, whose story is portrayed in the bestseller *A Gift of Prophecy,* is perhaps the most famous female false prophet. One of her most spine-tingling prophecies began the night of July 14, 1952. As she lay in bed waiting for the sun to rise, a serpentlike figure appeared and gently nudged her bed. Shaped like a garden hose, the serpent then coiled around her legs and hips. Dixon continues,

> The serpent turned its head and our eyes met. It [sic] eyes reflected all the wisdom and suffering of the ages, but also an unspoken plea for trust and understanding. It moved its head again, facing the East once more, as if to tell me that I must look to the East for wisdom and understanding. Somehow I sensed that it was conveying to me that if my trust and faith in it were great enough, I would be able to partake of its unlimited earthly wisdom.[25]

This first vision extended to three others, with the last taking place on February 5, 1962, when she saw a baby clothed in ragged garments held by Queen Nefertiti, an ancient queen of Egypt. Dixon watched as Nefertiti was stabbed in the back, and when she looked again the child had grown to manhood and all nations worshiped him. This child, she claims, was born in the Middle East the same day of her vision. He is a descendant of Nefertiti, whose influence would be felt in the 1980s, and by 1999 he would rule the world. The child, she claims, is the antichrist.[26]

Dixon has made numerous false prophecies. She predicted that China would join the United Nations in 1959, and that Russia would invade Iran in 1953, then invade Palestine in 1957, and also be the first nation to land humans on the moon. The war in Vietnam would be over in 1966, and Richard Nixon would not resign from the presidency.[27]

Perhaps Dixon's most famous "true" prediction forecasted the election and assassination of John F. Kennedy. But these predictions were also flawed. Although she predicted a blue-eyed Democrat would become president in 1960, she later predicted Nixon's victory for that same year.[28] Of course, even if she had not predicted Nixon's victory there is nothing supernatural about taking a risk on the fifty-fifty chance that a Democrat would win the presidency. And Dixon predicted only that the president would *die* in office, not specifically that he would be assassinated.[29] Since six out of the previous twenty-five presidents had died in office, Dixon had a roughly one-in-four chance of being right. Not a bad play in poker.

Even though Jeane Dixon teaches false doctrine, consults horoscopes and uses occult objects such as a crystal ball, certain Catholics and Protestants respect her prophecies![30] Without mentioning her by name, Edgar Whisenant promotes Dixon's antichrist predictions, which are already turning out false since there was no political leader in his twenties who greatly influenced world politics in the 1980s.[31]

Since she has offered an endless barrage of prophecies, don't be surprised if some of Dixon's predictions come true. This has more to do with luck than with a gift of prophecy. If you throw enough rotten peaches against a wall, some of them are bound to stick.

Reason 57: David Koresh Was Not the Messiah

On February 28, 1993, the Bureau of Alcohol, Tobacco and Firearms (ATF), a division of the U.S. Treasury Department, stormed a cult compound in Waco, Texas. The operation failed, and a standoff followed. After fifty-one days, the Federal Bureau of Investigation, having taken over the case, placed the compound under siege on April 19. A fire broke out, quickly engulfing the entire structure. In the end, about eighty cult members and at least seventeen children were dead.

Vernon Howell, the leader of the Branch Davidians—an offshoot of the Seventh-day Adventists—had changed his name to David Koresh in 1990. According to former Branch Davidian David Bunds, Koresh derived his name from Ezekiel 34 and 37, which predict that a messianic figure called David will reign over the future kingdom of Israel. Koresh believed himself to be the fulfillment of this prophecy. Combining the name David with Cyrus (*koresh* in Hebrew)—Cyrus being the anointed shepherd in Isaiah 44:28 to 45:1—Howell found his new name. David Koresh then claimed to be the little lamb of Isaiah

16, then the Lamb mentioned in Revelation 5. Finally, he openly declared himself to be the Second Coming of Christ.[32]

After gaining absolute control over the sect in 1989, Koresh dissolved marriages so that he could marry any woman in the commune. He promised that all his wives would repopulate the world with his seed.

What does martyrdom mean to a man who thought he was Christ? Koresh believed he would rise again from the dead and destroy the United States system, which was the whore of Babylon. Some surviving members of the cult believe he did rise immediately after the Waco holocaust. They await his coming in the clouds.

Jesus said many would come in his name saying "I am the Christ" and deceive many (Mt 24:4-5). This prophecy applies to the entire New Testament era (2 Pet 2:1-3). Throughout history many have claimed to be the Messiah. In 1534 Jan Bockelson, alias John of Leyden, declared that he was the Messiah and that the Westphalian city of Munster was the New Jerusalem. Like Koresh, he was young and charismatic and could demand sex from any female in his community. Like Waco, Munster ended in tragedy. In September 1535, Catholic authorities, having besieged the city, massacred the starving Munster community and paraded Bockelson with two of his leaders throughout neighboring towns. Then, having tortured them, authorities hung Bockelson and his officers in cages—a feast for the fowls of the air. In Westphalia the cages remain a tourist attraction to this day.[33]

Until Christ returns, messiahs and madmen are here to stay. Nevertheless, we can guard ourselves and others from false prophets by comparing their beliefs and actions with Scripture. Unlike false messiahs, Christ will return visibly, and "every eye will see him" (Rev 1:7; see also Mt 24:26-27; Acts 1:11). Furthermore, the true Messiah would never contradict his former teachings and moral standards. Nor would he have anything to do with psychological manipulation or sexual promiscuity. The prophetic David in Ezekiel 34 and 37 is Jesus Christ himself, not David Koresh.

Jesus, the suffering servant in Isaiah and the Lamb of God in Revelation, is the real Messiah who bore our sins on the cross. Anyone who claims to be the Messiah had better have Christ's crucifixion marks to prove it.

9
Reasons Why
No One
<u>Knows the Date</u>
<u>Through Sources</u>
<u>Outside the Bible</u>

*A*mid the late-night dregs on television emerges a "Call 900" number for psychics. The commercial assures us that our fortunes will not be read by some fly-by-night psychic, only by those who are certified by the American Association of Professional Psychics. Clearly, Christians are not the only ones who are predicting the future. One psychic called Criswell also predicts the end of the world in 1999.

But just like evangelical date-setters, Criswell has already missed the mark, having predicted the outbreak of a second U.S. civil war by the end of the 1970s, the unprecedented sales of a book entitled *The Cannibal Cookbook* in that same decade, the suicide of a U.S. president in 1980 and the emergence of the lost continent of Atlantis from the Atlantic Ocean in 1987.[1]

After Christmas, go to the local magazine stand and pick up one of the tabloids predicting next year's events. Then wrap it up with a "Do Not Open Till Christmas" label. When next Christmas arrives, open the package and read the magazine. Chances are that 95 percent of its predictions have proved false.

Strangely, sometimes Bible-believing Christians appeal to sources outside the Bible to confirm their prophecies. Televangelist Jack Van Impe has mastered the art of citing non-Christian sources that coincide with his end-time views. In this chapter we'll look at some of the most common nonbiblical sources.

Reason 58: New Age and Occult Literature Make False Predictions

Many New Agers find the year 2000 significant. They say the new millennium will usher in the age of Aquarius, in which all duality (any conception of opposites, including good and evil, life and death) will cease.[2] This is not the first time an astrological sign has been incorporated into a doomsday prediction. During the Third Crusade, an astrologer in Spain named John of Toledo forecast that a great catastrophe would devastate the earth in A.D. 1186. Christians fearfully heeded his prediction, which failed to materialize.[3]

Receiving messages from the stars or channelers or psychics or any other occult means is absolutely forbidden by Scripture (Deut 18:9-13; Is 47:13-14; Gal 5:19-21). Christians have no business using occult sources to confirm their predictions. And be wary of scaremongers who cite New Age sources as "proof" that an antichrist conspiracy will take over the world by a proposed date. New Age predictions, like most other predictions, will prove wrong. If God has not chosen to give the date to his followers, why would he offer it to his enemies?

Reason 59: UFO Enthusiasts Do Not Know the Date of the End

Many cults, such as the Jehovah's Witnesses, have claimed that their group represents the 144,000 chosen saints in Revelation 7. Now UFO devotees claim the same thing. They speak of Armageddon, the reign of antichrist, Elijah's return and, of course, the time of the Second Coming—which they believe will happen sometime around A.D. 2005.[4] One UFO sect headed by Solara Antara Amaa-ra claimed the 144,000 must be accounted for by January 11, 1992, to enter into a new golden era. Since that date failed, the next opportunity will be on December 31, 2011.[5]

UFO groups claim to receive messages from extraterrestrials. More likely, the alleged aliens are dreamed up by their channelers. If there is some external force behind these messages, they are probably not aliens but what the Bible calls demons. One theme that is common in the messages of such "aliens" is the denial that Jesus is God incarnate. They also affirm that all paths lead to God. Both teachings are diametrically opposed to Scripture (see Jn 1:1-14; 14:6; Acts 4:12). Like Solara's 1992 prediction, UFO doomsday dates will no doubt fail.

Reason 60: Calendars Do Not Give the Correct Date for the End

New Age author Jose Arguelles, in his book called *The Mayan Factor,* called for 144,000 to join together in certain locations such as the pyramids and Mount Shasta on August 16-17, 1987, for a "harmonic convergence" that would usher in the New Age and avert Armageddon. According to the ancient Mayan culture's calendar, the present era will end in A.D. 2012.[6]

Date-setters often exploit ancient calendars. Christian prophecy pundit Robert W. Faid claims that archaeologists have recently discovered an Egyptian calendar dating back to 4000 B.C. This calendar, based on solar years, allegedly runs out in A.D. 2001. This is the same year, Faid asserts, that the Mayan calendar ends.[7]

Now Faid and Arguelles cannot both be right about the Mayan calendar. There is obviously some manipulation of the calendar dates.

But why should we accept the Mayan or Egyptian calendar? Why not accept the Hindu calendar that gives us at least another forty million years before the world is recycled? The reason is self-evident: the Hindu calendar suggests that the world will not end in our lifetime.

There is no reason to assume the Mayans, Hindus, Persians or any other cultures know the date of the end when Christ himself did not know it (Mk 13:32).

Reason 61: The Pyramids Do Not Give the Correct Date for the End

Doomsday dates are sometimes derived by calculating the lengths of the chambers within a pyramid. Like all mathematical calculations supposedly pointing to the end, the numbers can be manipulated by anyone to defend virtually any date. The Jehovah's Witnesses, under Charles Taze Russell, discovered that the measurements of the Great Pyramid allegedly pointed to 1914 for the return of Christ. With a little help from the pyramid, David Webber and Noah Hutchings suggested that the tribulation would begin somewhere between 1981 to 1985. Later their date was changed to 1988.[8] Reginald Dunlop claimed the pyramid pointed to a final date of September 23, 1994.[9]

When Christians use pyramids to justify their predictions, they implicitly agree with heretical groups like the Mormons and Jehovah's Witnesses, as well as Satanists and Anglo-Israeli racists, that the Great Pyramid hides secret truths. The array of dates taught by prophecy aficionados demonstrate that no one has a corner on the truth regarding predictions from the pyramid. Any date is fair game, since pyramidologists can calculate by inches, feet, cubits, yards or any such measurement in order to arrive at a presumed date. French scholar Maurice Bouisson demonstrated this by counting the number of steps and landings in the Eiffel Tower (1,927) and subtracting the number of men at the Lord's Supper to get 1914.[10]

The Bible makes it clear that no one, not even a pyramidologist, knows the time of Christ's return.

Reason 62: The Prophecies of Nostradamus Are Not Accurate

The Japanese messiah has arrived. In Yokohama, Ryuho Okawa preaches before his congregation, claiming to be the reincarnation of Buddha. Actually he boasts: "I came here as more than the Messiah. . . . This universe, this world were based on my words and my teachings."[11] His Institute for Research in Human Happiness has grown to two million members. According to his book *Nostradamus: Fearful Prophecies,* Okawa believes that in the twenty-first century Japan will survive the end of the world, destroying both the United States and Russia. China will then become Japan's slave, and Korea its prostitute.

In Los Angeles County on May 10, 1988, the Griffith Observatory received hundreds of calls from people who were worried that Los Angeles would suffer a great earthquake that day. Their fears were largely based on a 1981 movie narrated by Orson Welles called *The Man Who Saw Tomorrow.* The film had mythologized the medieval sage Nostradamus, who had predicted a major quake would devastate "the new city" one May when certain planets and stars moved into a precise alignment. The alignment was due to occur on May 10, 1988. The film interpreted the city to be San Francisco or Los Angeles.[12]

Who was Nostradamus? Michel de Notredame (1503-1566) was a French physician whose Jewish parents converted to Christianity. Having studied the Jewish Cabala and the stars, he became the court seer for Catherine de Medici, queen of France. His most famous prophetic work (published around 1555) was called *The Centuries.* The book is categorized into quatrains (four-line verses) written in medieval French rhymes and deliberately vague. Nostradamus allegedly predicted that Henry II would be killed, pierced through the eye while jousting. Here is the prophetic stanza (*Century I,* quatrain 35):

> The young lion will overcome the old one
> On the field of battle in single combat:
> He will put out his eyes in a cage of gold:
> Two fleets one, then to die a cruel death.

The word *fleets* must be reinterpreted as "fractures" or "wounds."[13] But there was only one wound, and the lance pierced the king's brain, not his eye. Also, Henry's helmet was not gold.

Nostradamus also supposedly predicted three antichrists: Napoleon, Hitler and the future antichrist named Mabus, the great "King of Terror" who will be of Arabian descent, will wear a blue turban and will come to power in 1999. World War III will start around 1994, lasting twenty-seven years. New York will be devastated by nuclear bombs during this war.[14]

All of Nostradamus's prophecies are ambiguous enough to interpret a number of different ways. A conspiracy behind the death of John F. Kennedy is interpreted from a phrase about a guilty person who lies "hidden in the misty woods." Nostradamus supposedly predicted Robert Kennedy's death with the phrase "Another falls in the night." Manipulating the ambiguous prophecies of *The Centuries,* Hitler's minister of propaganda produced forged leaflets of Nostradamus's prophecies predicting Germany's victory in World War II. Great Britain and the United States responded with Nostradamus tracts of their own.

Did the medieval seer really predict the rise of Napoleon and Hitler? Napoleon is rendered from quatrain 8.1, which begins with "PAU, NAY, LORON." These are the names of three neighboring cities in southwestern France. There is no reason to assume Nostradamus had Napoleon in mind. Hitler is interpreted from "Hister," who is with the "German child" in the quatrain 2.24.[15] Once again, the facts seem distorted. Hister is actually an old name for part of the Danube River in Europe, and "German" is *germain* in French, which means "brother" or "first cousin."[16] The quatrain has nothing to do with Hitler or World War II.

It seems that the only prophecies of Nostradamus that "come true" are discovered *after* the events take place—and this means that his followers are manipulating his predictions. Why didn't we hear about Nostradamus's prediction of the manner of Kennedy's assassination *prior* to 1963? Whenever Nostradamus-interpreters stick their necks out by predicting an event in the future, the predictions fail. According to *The Man Who Saw Tomorrow,* Ted Kennedy would win the presidential election in 1984 and a worldwide famine would occur in the 1980s. No devastating earthquake occurred in 1988, and World War III will not break out in 1994.

James Randi, who wrote *The Mask of Nostradamus,* discovered a medieval document in which Catherine writes that Nostradamus predicted that her godfather Conetable, as well as her son Charles, would both live to the ripe age of ninety. History records Conetable's death at seventy-seven and Charles's death at only twenty-four.[17] Randi claims that in 103 cases in which Nostradamus specifically mentions persons, dates or other falsifiable data, he was wrong 100 percent of the time.[18]

Finally, Nostradamus's means of prophesying conflicted with Scripture. He went into trances, consulted horoscopes and used other forms of divination (Deut 18). By Scripture's standards, his false prophecies make him a false prophet. Despite these grave erros, some evangelicals like Jack Van Impe actually claim that it's okay to quote Nostradamus on prophecy. He was "a great Bible student"![19]

Reason 63: The Dead Sea Scrolls Do Not Give Us a Date for the End

The Dead Sea Scrolls have sparked controversy ever since their discovery in 1947. The scrolls were found in several caves; some date back to about 200 B.C., and all bear witness to the early age of Old Testament and Jewish writings.

One scroll discovered in 1952 was made from copper and thus is known as the Copper Scroll. Unlike all the other scrolls, the Copper Scroll appears to be an ancient treasure map. This map, Grant Jeffrey suggests, leads to the burial site of the gold and silver instruments found in the old Jewish temple. Once uncovered, these instruments will be used for the new temple in Jerusalem.[20] Vendyl Jones, founder of the Institute for Judaic Christian Research, who claims to be the person on whom the movie character Indiana Jones is based, believes the Copper Scroll will help him track down the ashes of the red heifer, which are needed for temple worship.[21]

Does the Copper Scroll give the whereabouts of the instruments in the temple? Archaeologist J. T. Milik, one of the foremost authorities on the scrolls, believes the information in the Copper Scroll is mythical. And even if the scroll did inform us where the temple instruments could be found, this does not mean we would find them. Over the process of hundreds of years they could have disintegrated, or robbers could have stolen them. If we were to find such a treasure, it is inconceivable that any of these vessels—now ancient, priceless and frail— would be subjected to the risk of being damaged by use in a future temple. At any rate, none of the Dead Sea Scrolls give us any hint regarding the date of the Second Coming.

Reason 64: Jewish Sources Do Not Give the Correct Date for the End

Another popular ploy of date-setters is to quote Jewish rabbis who believe the Messiah will come around A.D. 2000. J. R. Church cites Rabbi Ben Zion Wacholder and Rashi, while Jack Van Impe cites Rabbi Elias, Rabbi Katina, Rabbi Schneerson and the book of Enoch.[22]

But Jews who are faithful to their calendar start their history at 3761 B.C.; this makes A.D. 2000 the year 5760-5761, an insignificant date. The year 2000 bears no spiritual significance for Jewish scholars. Date-setters can always find fringe Jewish teachers who consider the year 2000 significant, just as they can find fringe Jewish groups promoting the rebuilding of the temple; but such predictions are not accepted by mainstream Jews.

The book of Enoch predicts a six-thousand-year date, but there is no evidence that the end of the six thousand years comes at A.D. 2000. Moreover, this book was not written by the Enoch mentioned in Genesis 5. Technically called 2 Enoch (32-33), it was written as late as A.D. 1000 and has never been considered an inspired work.[23] It wields no prophetic authority among either Jews or Christians.

A final point: if the Jews cannot recognize Jesus as their Messiah, what makes us think some Jews' expectation of a messianic coming in A.D. 2000 is accurate? Followers of the late Rabbi Schneerson claimed he was the Messiah! Van Impe might as well have supported his end-time dates from the messages of Branch Davidian leader David Koresh, another alleged messiah.

Reason 65: The Appearances of Mary Are Misleading

Shots rang out on May 13, 1981, at St. Peter's Square before seventy-five thousand people. While stooping over to bless a little girl holding a picture of the Lady Fatima, Pope John Paul II was shot by Mehmet Ali Agca, a man reportedly linked to the KGB, the former Soviet Union's secret-service agency. After the Pope recovered, he believed it was the Virgin Mary who saved him, and he paid a visit to an aging Carmelite nun named Lucia, the surviving visionary of Fatima in Portugal. No one really knows what they talked about, but after the visit the Pope consecrated the Soviet Union to the Virgin. In 1991 communism fell in the Soviet states.

While revolution raged in Russia in 1917, three peasant children in Portugal named Lucia dos Santos, Jacinta and Francisco de Jesus Marto claimed to have seen the Virgin Mary on six separate occasions from May 13 to October 13. Over fifty thousand people witnessed a sign from the final appearance of Fatima. One reporter from the secular press described the event. After the rain clouds parted,

the sun—like a shining disc of dull silver—appeared at its full zenith, and began to whirl around in a violent and wild dance, that a large number of people likened to a carnival display, with such lovely glowing colours passing successively over the sun's surface. A miracle, as the crowd cried out; or a supernatural phenomenon,

as the learned say? It is not important for me to know the answer
now, but only to tell you and confirm what I saw.[24]
The children were given three visions. The first was a vision of hell,
predicting the end of World War I. The second predicted World War
II and the danger of communist Russia. If enough people prayed and
if Russia were consecrated to the Virgin, Christianity would overtake
communism in Russia. The final vision, though scheduled to be read
in 1960, was never revealed because Pope John XXIII thought it not
advisable. Nevertheless, an extract from the third message appeared
in *Neues Europa,* a respected newspaper from Stuttgart, Germany, on
October 1, 1963, and was given to U.S. president John F. Kennedy,
British prime minister Harold Macmillan and Soviet leader Nikita
Khrushchev.[25] Part of the extract reads:

What I have already made known at La Salette through the children Melanie and Maximin, I repeat today before you. Mankind
has not developed as God expected. Mankind has been sacrilegious
and has trampled underfoot the gifts which were given it. . . . If
those at the top in the world and in the church do not oppose these
acts, it is I who shall do so, and I shall pray God My Father to
VISIT HIS JUSTICE ON MEN. Then it is that God will punish
men, more harshly and more severely THAN HE PUNISHED
THEM BY THE FLOOD, and the great and powerful shall perish
thereby as well as the small and weak. There will also come a time
of the hardest trials for the Church. Cardinals will be against Cardinals, and bishops against bishops. Satan will put himself in their
midst. In Rome, also, there will be big changes. . . . The Church
will be darkened and the world plunged into confusion. THE BIG,
BIG WAR WILL HAPPEN IN THE SECOND HALF OF THE
TWENTIETH CENTURY. Then fire and smoke will fall from the
sky and the waters of the oceans will be turned to steam—hurling
their foam towards the sky; and all that is standing will be overthrown. Millions and more millions of men will lose their lives from
one hour to the next; and those who remain living at that moment

will envy those who are dead.

How do we assess such a prophecy? Not everyone in the Catholic church agrees that this extract is genuine, but many still identify it as the third secret.[26] According to Catholic insider and historian Malachi Martin, the pope currently fears that after he is gone the Vatican might give way to liberalism, causing a great apostasy.[27] Other messages allegedly from the Virgin Mary predict the same thing.[28]

Yet there have been false predictions in messages said to have come from the Virgin. In fact, the Lady of La Salette—mentioned favorably in the third vision of Fatima—predicted that the antichrist would be born around 1865.[29] Unless this antichrist is still alive (which would make him about 130 years old), we can safely affirm this was a false prophecy. What does that say about the third vision of Fatima as reported by the *Neues Europa?*

It's difficult to deny the miracle performed by the Lady Fatima in 1917. But Scripture tells us that many false prophets will arise to do great signs and wonders, causing fire to come down from heaven, as was the case in 1917. And Satan is always capable of masquerading as an angel of light (Mt 24:24; 2 Cor 11:14-15; Rev 13:11-13).

Having visited Medjudgorje, Yugoslavia, the location of another supposed appearance of Mary, research specialist Ken Samples gives his evaluation of the miracles:

When did Jesus ever make the sun dance or crosses spin? . . . Many miracles associated with Marian apparitions [vision-appearances of Mary] seem dramatic and sensational—attention-getting if you will—the kind of miracles that Jesus consistently *refused* to perform (Matt. 12:38-39). This is a good reason to at least suspect the source of these miracles. . . . I am convinced that millions of people . . . actually worship the Virgin—perhaps ignorantly, and certainly against official church teaching. This is idolatry. Where there is idolatry, satanic activity is certain (1 Cor. 10:14-22).[30]

People who desperately want to know the future but are not satisfied with the Bible's prophecies can easily fall into consulting visions,

UFOs, astrology, calendars, the writings of soothsayers or any other means to satisfy their curiosity. But predictions obtained through these avenues also prove false and often lead their inquirers away from the kingdom of God and closer to the kingdom of Satan.

10
Reasons Why No One Knows the Date Through Rumors

*E*nd-time predictors tend to use one of three methods for deriving their prophecies. I call the first of these "Cabala theology." Popularized by the medieval Jewish mystics, this method finds a hidden meaning behind every passage of Scripture. As we have seen already, however, calculating dates for the end based on the numbers of Scripture is totally unreliable.

I call the second method "newspaper theology." Prophecy speculators who prefer this method carry a Bible in one hand and a newspaper in the other, forever marrying them in prophetic wedlock. They seem to unravel a prophecy for every significant event in the headlines. Of course, Christians *should* evaluate the news from a biblical perspective. The problem comes when prophecy buffs begin to speculate or insist that events in the headlines fulfill specific prophecies.

A third method date-setters utilize is "comic-book theology," forever pitting good supernatural forces against evil. This sensationalistic approach normally combines science fiction with the supernatural, playing on rumors, unexplained events and unsolved mysteries. This chapter examines the problems with using rumors for end-time speculation.

A rumor may be defined as an unauthenticated story passed along mostly by word of mouth. When someone tries to verify the story or to find eyewitnesses, no hard evidence is uncovered—only hype, hearsay and hasty generalizations. Here is a list of some of the most prominent ones in prophecy.

Reason 66: Stories of Vanishing Hitchhikers Are Rumors

Once upon a time, on a freeway far, far away, two Christian women were driving home when they noticed a male hitchhiker on the shoulder of the road. For some reason they felt compelled to pick up this man, even though they normally never picked up male hitchhikers. The man spoke to them about the Second Coming, then placed his hand on the driver's shoulder and said, "He's coming sooner than you think." Continuing at a speed of about 55 miles per hour, the women turned their heads to find no one in the back seat. They pulled over and began to praise God for this angelic visitation. When a police officer stopped to ask if they needed assistance, the women related the event to him. To their surprise, the officer claimed they were the umpteenth witnesses of the angel.

I have heard this rumor preached from the pulpit as "gospel truth." This rumor falls under the category of "urban myth"—a tale of strange happenings that is told and retold mostly among people in cities. There are many versions of the prophetic-hitchhiker story. The tale dates back to at least 1876, with the witnesses riding by horse and carriage. One writer named Brian Finn pursued dozens of these claims but could not find anyone who had actually seen or met the vanishing hitchhiker.[1]

Reason 67: Stories of a Coming New Jerusalem Asteroid Are Unfounded

A dazzling bright object called SS 433 is allegedly traveling to earth at thirty thousand miles per second. Right now it's about ten thousand light-years away. According to Southwest Radio Church, this may be the New Jerusalem.[2] Similarly, Jack Van Impe suggests that a coming white light is Jesus, the light of the world returning to earth! What astronomers now call the Northern Wall is the New Jerusalem that is to descend from heaven (Rev 21).[3]

Such stories are normally cited from scientific magazines but grossly taken out of context by the prophecy teachers. Then they are passed on orally by overzealous prophecy students. One might ask, If the New Jerusalem is ten thousand light-years away, even going at the speed of light, how will it get to the earth before ten thousand years from now? That is a bit longer than most prophecy students want to wait.

But if the New Jerusalem is a heavenly city, as Scripture teaches, it transcends the material universe as does the resurrected Christ. In other words, Christ and the New Jerusalem are not limited by space and time. Neither the New Jerusalem nor Christ needs to travel through space over a period of a certain number of years to get to earth.

Reason 68: Bees and Vultures Are Not Currently Fulfilling Prophecy

Every so often we hear stories of killer bees from South America or Africa that are making their way to the United States. The stories are then connected to prophecy (Rev 6:8; 9:1-11). A series of attacks by African killer bees—which were being used to produce honey—occurred in Houston, Texas, in November 1993. The bees reportedly killed some household pets and livestock. But the animals had been tied on a leash or in some other way trapped outside, so that they had nowhere to hide as the bees swarmed and relentlessly stung them. Since humans are not tied outside on ropes or chains, it is highly unlikely that any people will be killed by such bees.

A similar story has to do with an explosion in the population of vultures or other scavenger birds in Palestine.[4] They are supposedly waiting for the Battle of Armageddon so they can fulfill their end-time role by eating the flesh of untold millions of human carcasses (Ezek 39:17-20; Rev 19:17-18). Actually, birds migrate annually to the Jerusalem area, but this does not mean they are preparing for Armageddon.

Reason 69: Stories of Hell's Enlarging Itself Are Unfounded

Sometimes rumors focus on volcanoes that Christians connect with Isaiah 5:14: "hell hath enlarged herself" (KJV). This verse is then projected into the future as a sign of the end times. But this interpretation requires us to accept the misguided notion that hell is in the center of the earth. All *hell* means in Isaiah 5:14 is "the grave," as any modern translation will demonstrate.

Other times the Bermuda Triangle—also called the Devil's Triangle—is rumored to be the gateway to hell via UFO kidnappings or an underground water shaft. Yet tales of mysterious disappearances in the Bermuda Triangle are really rumors rather than mysteries. Most of the vanishing ships or aircraft disappear during the storm season. Remember the tragic disaster of the *Columbia* space shuttle in 1986? Very little of the wreckage was recovered after the flying debris hit the ocean. Many things can get lost in the sea, especially during a storm or when a ship explodes. Other Bermuda Triangle accounts are simply fiction or distortion of facts, including the famed Rosalie, V. A. Fogg and DC-3 plane disappearances.[5]

Another rumor was promoted on TBN's *Praise the Lord* program when evangelist R. W. Shambach told Paul Crouch that scientists in Siberia had drilled a hole nine miles into the earth and realized that they'd discovered hell when they heard human voices crying in pain. (How could molten lava disturb the immaterial souls of lost humans?)

Rich Buhler's investigation of this rumor led him on a wild-goose chase until he met up with Age Rendalen, the man responsible for first sending TBN the article about hell. Rendalen claimed: "I fabricated every word of it! . . . The story is nothing more than a Christian 'urban legend' without basis in reality"6

Reason 70: Stories That Social Security Is in League with the Mark of the Beast Are Unfounded

A popular rumor tells of a couple who reportedly received a check from the Social Security Administration by accident. These checks carried a message to the effect of "Do not cash without the proper identifying mark on the right hand or forehead." When Social Security officials got wind of the fact that such a check had been mailed, they allegedly said, "These checks are not supposed to come out until 1984." Mary Stewart Relfe quoted this rumor (which she believed was true) from an evangelist by the name of Darrell Dunn.7 The rumor dissipated, of course, after 1984.

Still, similar rumors find their way into the Christian community. Another was started in the early 1990s, instigated by a billboard sign depicting the universal product code on the forehead of a person. The billboard was cited as "proof" that the mark of the Beast had arrived! The sign really existed, but no mark of the Beast resulted from it.

Such stories appeal to our itching ears. The Bible encourages us to think critically and to test everything we hear (Acts 17:11; 1 Thess 5:21).

Reason 71: The Procter & Gamble Company Is Not Satanist

As Danny and Rachel selected groceries at the supermarket, they inspected each product with great care to see if it bore the logo of a half-moon with thirteen stars. They did not want to buy any product with that mark, because it came from Procter & Gamble. Their pastor had preached last Sunday morning that this company, along with

McDonald's, was run by Satanists.

By far one of the most damaging rumors that have spread through the Christian community is that the president of Procter & Gamble appeared on *Phil Donahue* claiming to have sold his soul to the devil. Some versions have him on *Merv Griffin* or *60 Minutes*. The stars on the Procter & Gamble logo reportedly are arranged to represent "666."

For over a decade Procter & Gamble spent vast amounts of money to fight this rumor. Why would the company head have announced on national television that he is a Satanist, knowing the company would lose sales if he did so? The rumor simply doesn't add up. Fed up with the persistent rumor, the company filed a lawsuit against a couple in Topeka, Kansas; they were convicted of spreading "false and malicious statements" and had to pay Procter & Gamble seventy-five thousand dollars. Christians who wish to perpetuate the slanderous rumor should be aware that Procter & Gamble will fight in court for their protection—and judges and juries will not accept rumors and hearsay as evidence.

What about the moon-and-stars logo? The thirteen stars represent the original thirteen states of the United States, not 666.

Reason 72: Evidence of a New Age Conspiracy Is Lacking

Theosophist Alice Baily, the founder of Lucis Trust, introduced "The Plan" in the 1930s, anticipating a takeover of the entire world by the New Age movement, with the unveiling of Lord Maitreya as the antichrist. So writes Constance Cumbey in her bestseller *The Hidden Dangers of the Rainbow*. This New Age conspiracy is reportedly being fulfilled exactly as planned.

Many Christians believe the New Age movement will be that end-time religion embraced by the antichrist. After all, don't New Agers like Shirley MacLaine believe they themselves are God? Isn't this the blasphemous claim of the coming antichrist (2 Thess 2:1-5)?

Yes, it is, but this does not necessarily mean the New Age movement is the prophesied end-time religion. The antichrist will certainly claim to be God, but to the exclusion of all other claims of deity (look again at 2 Thess 2:1-5). In that case, pantheism (the New Age belief that all is God, including oneself) may not be the religion of the antichrist, for he will not permit anyone else to be God.

Is there really a New Age conspiracy? This is highly unlikely. The New Age movement is not a tightly knit group, but a network of occultists with no central base or leader. More important, New Agers disagree on many issues. While Maitreya promoter Benjamin Creme believes that Lord Maitreya will rule the world, prominent New Agers like Marilyn Ferguson consider this idea ludicrous. She, like many other New Agers, is awaiting a "Cosmic Christ," not a literal Maitreya messiah.

The New Age "harmonic convergence" in the late 1980s would supposedly begin a five-year "plan" to establish the New Age messiah and dissolve the United States and all of Christendom.[8] Now that 1993 has passed, we can safely say that claim was false.

Even those who may consciously attempt to fulfill biblical prophecy *cannot do so* unless the Lord permits. God the Father has appointed the events in the end times, and humans cannot help God fulfill them without his permission (see Acts 1:7; 2 Thess 2:6).

If Christians cannot figure out the date of the end, what makes them think New Agers or any other non-Christians know the date? Many Christian scaremongers seem to believe that the predictions of New Agers will definitely come to pass. But Christian date-setters, Satanists, witches, New Agers, Jews and Gentiles all have one thing in common—none of them knows when the end will come.

Reason 73: The Illuminati Conspiracy Lacks Evidence

Even countercult organizations like the Christian Research Institute do not escape rumormongering. The alleged former Jesuit Alberto Rivera accused CRI of being a pawn of the Vatican because the late

Walter Martin, the founder of CRI, questioned Rivera's testimony that appears in popular comic books printed by Chick Publications.[9] Rumors then spread that Martin was a secret agent of Rome, though neither he nor anyone else on the CRI staff was Roman Catholic.

Later, Texe Marrs accused CRI of not believing in prophecy or the mark of the Beast.[10] And if CRI was a pawn of the Vatican, then it would be connected to the end-time Illuminati conspiracy about to take over the world. Who is involved in this conspiracy, according to Marrs? Practically every powerful political figure from Bill Clinton to George Bush, practically every political group from the United Nations, the Council of Foreign Relations and the Trilateral Commission to the Bilderbergers and the Club of Rome, practically every banking group from the World Bank to multinational corporations, practically every secret society from Freemasonry to the Skull & Bones, practically every intelligence agency from the CIA and FBI to the Mafia, KGB and Communist Party, and of course, practically every religious group from the New Age movement to the Vatican.[11]

The Illuminati rumor has now continued for two centuries. Actually, an Illuminati was established on May 1, 1776, in the state of Bavaria by Adam Weishaupt, a former Jesuit and canon law professor at the University of Ingolstadt. The Illuminati was a German secret society within Masonic lodges. This group was definitely anti-Christian and did attempt to overthrow the kings of Europe. Prompted by the Jesuits, who saw the Illuminati as a threat, Elector Charles Theodore outlawed the group in 1785. After this the Illuminati faded into oblivion, only to be resurrected by Abbe Barruel and Scot John Robison toward the end of the eighteenth century. Both said that the Illuminati had masterminded the French Revolution. That is where the myth started. These claims, which postdate the breakup of the Illuminati, lack evidence and are highly improbable.[12]

The Illuminati rumor then traveled to America, promoted by a Boston preacher named Jedidiah Morse. From then on the rumor kept incorporating more groups, particularly any group considered dangerous. Every "bad boy" became fair game. During the nineteenth century the Jesuits, who had originally helped to outlaw the society, were accused of being coconspirators with the Masons. Anti-Semitic sentiments in the early twentieth century prompted conspiracy buffs to accuse the Zionists of being part of the Illuminati. One spurious paper linking the Jews to the Illuminati, "The Protocols of the Elders of Zion," circulated widely in German schools during the 1930s and 1940s.[13] Yet more recent perpetrators of the rumor never seem to include the Jews on their conspiracy list.

In the second half of the twentieth century Marxists, Satanists and the New Age movement were added to the growing list. John Todd, who claimed to be a former witch for the Illuminati, frightened gullible Christians into believing that the Illuminati was plotting to take over the world in October 1979. The Rothschild Tribunal had selected Jimmy Carter as the antichrist, and Charles Manson, with a band of other prisoners, would be released the same year and go on a Christian-killing rampage. Todd was later exposed as an emotionally disturbed fraud.

Apologist G. Richard Fisher lists twenty-six different Illuminati theories, many of which contradict each other.[14] And that's the heart of the problem. Because they are not based on hard fact, but on assumptions, hasty generalizations and faulty inferences drawn from shoddy evidence, rumors of Illuminati conspiracies are legion.

Conspiracy speculators misinterpret history and statements made by the people they wish to accuse. They read into the statements their own presuppositions and biases, then draw faulty conclusions. They *want* to believe that the Vatican, the Mormons, Bill Clinton, Nelson Rockefeller or the Christian Research Institute is part of a great conspiracy. Anything that contradicts their fantasy is written off as a "smokescreen." Anyone who criticizes them becomes part of the conspiracy.

Beware of claims that lack solid evidence from primary sources or are unverifiable, outrageous, sensationalistic or rejected by almost all

A brief list of supposed Illuminati conspirators

Promoter	Conspirators	Significance
(Correct account)	Adam Weishaupt and German Masons	The only true Illuminati conspiracy (1776-1785)
Eliphas Levi	Zoroaster and the Knights Templar	Persian origin; spread to Europe in the twelfth century
Chick Publications	A mysterious man in black	Gave Thomas Jefferson the seal of the Illuminati, which became the U.S. seal
Gerald Winrod	The Jews	Became Nazi propaganda
Lyndon LaRouche	British Masons through Knights of St. John of Malta	Reintroduced the Egyptian cult of Isis, influencing terrorists and cults
John Birch Society	Communism, Council of Foreign Relations, Rothschilds	World banker theory
High I.Q. Bulletin	Invaders from Venus	?
Robert Anton Wilson	ESP contacts from Sirius	Extraterrestrials implanted the idea of the Illuminati in human minds
John Todd	Masons, CFR, witches, Mafia	Jimmy Carter and Charles Manson said to be involved
Mike Warnke	Satanists	Hired assassins to bump off the Kennedys and M. L. King Jr.
Texe Marrs	Global conspiracy	Ready to take over the world and reveal the antichrist

discerning Christians (see Prov 11:14). Yes, scaremongers may wave before you some written words of prominent leaders allegedly confirming the conspiracy. But in what context were the statements made? What did the persons mean by what they said? Would they agree with the statement made about them? Do they still hold to the same position they are quoted as holding?

Many of us like thrilling movies, and sensational rumors have a similar thrill appeal. But such rumors are usually spread at the price of someone's reputation. The Bible speaks out very strongly against slander: those who practice it will not "inherit the kingdom of God" (1 Cor 6:10; compare 1 Cor 5:11; Eph 4:31). Let's be extremely cautious that we do not fulfill Paul's words: "For a time will come when they will not listen to wholesome instruction, but will overwhelm themselves with teachers to suit their whims and tickle their fancies, and they will turn from listening to the truth and wander off after fictions" (2 Tim 4:3-4 Goodspeed; compare 1 Tim 1:3-4; 4:6-7).

11
Reasons Why
No One
Yet Knows
<u>Who Is</u>
<u>the Antichrist</u>

*A*ustralian Bible teacher Leonard Sale Harrison had it all fig-
ured out. The late 1930s or early 1940s would bring the end
of the world. Benito Mussolini was clearly the antichrist, for
the Italian dictator mimicked Julius Caesar by declaring that he was
the state. He called himself "superman incarnate," ruled as emperor
of a revived Rome and set about to make a huge image of himself.
His openness toward Protestantism made him a deceptive religious
man, and the Bank of America—originally the Bank of Italy—connected him with international economics.[1]

Christians in the time of World War II could point to other signs
as well: the apostasy of loose living in the 1920s, the immorality of
Hollywood in the 1930s, the Scopes Trials challenging the six days of
creation, the increase of technology, earthquakes such as the one in

Long Beach, California, in 1933 and another in Quetta, India, in 1935—the latter killing fifty thousand people—famine due to the Great Depression, various wars and rumors of wars, and of course World War II. And if the antichrist wasn't Mussolini, then it *had* to be Hitler.

A favorite pastime for prophecy speculators is determining the identity of the antichrist. Speculators who believe the antichrist lives today usually get sucked into date-setting. If the antichrist is alive, the end must come within our lifetime. Suppose the antichrist reached his fortieth birthday in 1994. This would mean the Great Tribulation will take place by about 2024, with 2034 as the most extreme limit for the end. Thus a date for the end is implicitly set.

Catholic author Emmet Culligan agrees with Jeane Dixon that the antichrist was born in 1962.[2] Christian visionary Raymond Aguilera believes the "last big War" will be fought in our lifetime, for "the day of the Beast is here."[3] The Arab Christian prophet Om Saleem claimed that the antichrist was born November 23, 1933, that his unveiling would come in 1993 and the rapture in 1994.[4] Not far behind, evangelical author Dave Hunt writes, "SOMEWHERE, AT THIS VERY MOMENT, on planet Earth, the Antichrist is almost certainly alive—biding his time, awaiting his cue."[5]

The key word for this chapter is *evidence*. What substantial evidence do we have for claiming that someone is the antichrist, or that the antichrist is alive today? About as much evidence as Harrison had for Mussolini. If Christians look hard enough, they are bound to find signs that point to the end. Next comes the antichrist guessing-game. Let's look at some recent and not-so-recent blunders.

Reason 74: There Is No Evidence That Any President of the United States Is the Antichrist

If you count the letters of the name Ronald Wilson Reagan, you will discover the pattern 6, 6, 6. The address of Reagan's California mansion also totaled 666. Some Christians suspected that Reagan was the antichrist. But Reagan professed to be a Christian. He insisted that the number of his address, given to him by his friends, be changed to 668. At one time he himself had been a prophecy speculator, claiming the Soviet Union was Gog and Magog.[6] But end-time speculators shrugged this evidence off as a smoke screen to hide Reagan's real agenda. What could be craftier than for the antichrist to masquerade as a conservative Christian?

Before Reagan there was Jimmy Carter. He was the antichrist because of his involvement with the Trilateral Commission. This same Carter also popularized the Christian phrase *born again* in the 1970s and banned drinking from the White House. What has this purported antichrist been doing since his presidency ended? He leads a Sunday-school class in his hometown in Georgia!

Every president since Carter has taken part in the Trilateral Commission or the Council of Foreign Relations; in any case, no president seems to escape accusations. For John F. Kennedy, it was his Roman Catholic religion and the 666 votes he received at the Democratic convention in 1956. For George Bush, it was his famed New World Order speeches and compromises with the Russian enemy. For Bill Clinton, it was his paradoxical claim to be Christian while supporting gay and abortion rights.

Even those running for president cannot escape accusations. Pat Robertson, who tried for the Republican nomination in 1988 and who once predicted Armageddon in 1982 and suggested the antichrist's birth around 1954, was himself accused of being the antichrist by Constance Cumbey.[7]

Slander knows no end. Needless to say, all presidential candidates for the antichrist have failed.

Reason 75: There Is No Evidence That Henry Kissinger Is the Antichrist

Henry Kissinger has been another favorite candidate for the antichrist. Why? He is a Jew, he is an American, and he was a diplomatic peacemaker. He also promotes a "new world order." His name in Hebrew adds up to 111, or 666 divided by 6. Starting with multiples of 6 (A=6, B=12, C=18, etc.) Salem Kirban—who wrote an entire book suggesting Kissinger was the antichrist—calculated Kissinger's last name at 666.[8] But now that the Nixon years are long behind us, the Kissinger-antichrist connection is getting old, and so is Kissinger.

Reason 76: There Is No Evidence That Pope John Paul II Is the Antichrist

Martin Luther thought the papacy was the antichrist, as did a host of other Reformers and Protestant leaders.[9] To this day, many Protestants still believe the pope is the antichrist, or at least the false prophet in Revelation 13.

Is there enough evidence to assume the pope is the antichrist? We must admit that the early Protestant leaders were wrong in at least one respect—the popes of their day were *not* the final antichrist, for those popes are now dead.

Nevertheless, it was a common Middle Age and Reformation practice to accuse one's persecutor of being the antichrist. Sometimes within the very ranks of Catholicism, the pope was accused of this ultimate heresy; Alexander IV (pope from 1254 to 1261) and Sylvester II (pope from 999 to 1003) were so charged. The papacy in its turn named Luther the antichrist. Radical Protestant Reformer Thomas Muntzer, of the Westphalian city of Munster, also claimed Luther was the antichrist.[10] With a bit of mathematical gymnastics and by rendering Luther's surname in Latin (Martin Lutera), an enemy of Luther could make the great Reformer's name total 666![11] Such accusations, of course, were no more valid than Luther's.

The Puritans called the Anglicans "the excrement of Antichrist." Both Archbishop of Canterbury William Laud and soldier/statesman Oliver Cromwell were accused of being the antichrist—their names allegedly adding up to 666. In America, Charles I of England was the antichrist, and during the Revolutionary War, King George III was given that infamous title. Americans "proved" his satanic role by cal-culating 666 from the phrase "Royal Supremacy in Great Britain" in both Greek and Hebrew.[12]

Ultimately, who gets accused of being the antichrist is relative to who has enemies. Since the pope has many enemies, he will often be given the title. But as was the case with the U.S. presidents, there is simply no substantial evidence that Pope John Paul II is the antichrist or false prophet. In fact, according to the biblical characteristics of the antichrist, the pope *cannot* be the antichrist. A denial that Jesus is the Christ associates one with "the spirit of the antichrist" (1 Jn 4:1-3; see also 1 Jn 2:22-23).

Reason 77: There Is No Evidence That Mikhail Gorbachev Is the Antichrist

"Gog is the leader of Russia. . . . Gorbachev's name in the original Russian language is GOGRBACHEV. Please note the first three let-ters."[13] Thus advised prophecy teacher Ron Reese to show how Gor-bachev's name is connected to Israel's end-time enemy Gog. (But Gog really isn't Russia, as I showed in reason 44.)

Some speculators think Mikhail Gorbachev is the prime candidate for the antichrist. In his book *Gorbachev! Has the Real Antichrist Come?* Robert Faid finds the ten final nations of the antichrist (Rev 13:1) to be Latvia, Estonia, Lithuania, Poland, Czechoslovakia, Hun-gary, Romania, East Germany, Bulgaria and Afghanistan. The wound the Beast suffers (Rev 13:3) is the breaking off of these nations from Russia, and the healing of the wound is the reunification of East and West Germany! Moreover, the eight successive kings in Revelation 17:10-11 are leaders of the Soviet Union: Lenin, Stalin, Malenkov, Khrushchev, Brezhnev, Andropov, Chernenko and Gorbachev. Gor-bachev even appeared in the "holy place" of the Vatican on December 1, 1989 (see 2 Thess 2:4). Finally, his name allegedly adds up to 1,332 (666 × 2) in both Russian and Hebrew.[14]

Before we start speculating whether the cells of Gorbachev's birthmark add up to 666, let's examine Faid's evidence. First, the 666 calculations are fixed. Remember, they really add up to 1,332, not 666. Additionally, the Russian calculation is based on the name Mikhail S. Gorbachev, not his full name—Mikhail Sergeevich Gorbachev. Faid then turns around and bases his Hebrew calculation on Mikhail Sergeevich Gorbachev instead of Mikhail S. Gorbachev! Moreover, the Hebrew transliteration Faid uses for Gorbachev's name is spelled wrong.[15] Second, Gorbachev did not declare himself to be God at the Vatican, nor would everyone consider the Vatican to be the "holy place" spoken of in 2 Thessalonians 2:4. Third, Faid skipped over the brief leadership of Bulganin (1955-1958), so the successive Soviet "kings" total nine, not eight, before the fall of communism.

In any case, after Boris Yeltsin became president of Russia, Gorbachev's candidacy for the antichrist began to fade.

Reason 78: There Is No Evidence That Saddam Hussein Is the Antichrist

"Because Babylon was built in ancient times, and was a great city, it must be a great city again in the time of our new great leader, Saddam Hussein." These pompous words were proclaimed by Shafqa Mohammed Jaafar, a prominent archaeologist in Iraq. Saddam Hussein—called the new Nebuchadnezzar in Iraq—has ordered the rebuilding of the ancient Babylonian king's original site. He has promised fifteen million dollars to anyone who can blueprint a plan for rebuilding the Babylonian Hanging Gardens, one of the seven wonders of the ancient world.[16]

If Hussein were to become the new Nebuchadnezzar portrayed as Lucifer in Isaiah 14, as newsletters like *The Voice of Elijah* suggest, it's easy to see why Christians would think he was the antichrist.[17] But it is highly unlikely that Revelation 17—18 refers to a literal reviving and destroying of the Babylonian empire. The city portrayed in Revelation is characterized by great wealth and busy trading, but Iraq, in spite of its oil, is not. And Saddam, wicked as he may be, does not declare himself to be God (2 Thess 2:4).

Reason 79: There Is No Evidence That Juan Carlos Is the Antichrist

The notion that Juan Carlos, king of Spain, is the antichrist has picked up momentum among prophecy speculators like Jack Van Impe and Joseph Aguilar.[18] But no one has slandered the Spanish monarch more than Charles Taylor, who wrote *The Antichrist King—Juan Carlos.* Taylor claimed that Juan Carlos—whose title will be "King of Jerusalem, Defender of Catholic Holy Lands Sites"—would not be revealed as the king of Europe until after the rapture. Somehow, though, Taylor seems to have been one of the chosen few who knew this secret in advance—but he would let us in on the secret if we were willing to pay $32.90 for his book and three cassettes on the subject.

Why is Juan Carlos a favored target? He is reportedly a direct descendant of Charles V, the Hapsburg emperor of the Holy Roman Empire. Hence it is anticipated that Carlos will be the emperor of the revived Roman Empire. Carlos also wields great influence in Latin America, making him a man of peace as the antichrist is expected to be. He is also called a friend of the Jew. And now that Spain is one of the nations in the European Community, Carlos will supposedly head this final end-time kingdom (Rev 13:1).

Such speculation gets us nowhere. There is no hard evidence that Spain will be the head of the EC in the near future, let alone that Juan Carlos will become its head. Anyone who knows history will recognize that Great Britain will not easily submit to Spain. And just as the Holy Roman Empire ended without the appearance of the antichrist, so the EC may one day break up without his appearance. There's simply no real evidence that Juan Carlos is the antichrist.

Reason 80: There Is No Evidence That Lord Maitreya Is the Antichrist

In the *Los Angeles Times,* an ad from the Tara Center read, "THE

CHRIST IS NOW HERE." Christ reappeared as an educator beginning in July 1977. He is called Lord Maitreya, the Second Coming of Christ, the fifth Buddha, Islam's Mahdi and the Hindus' Krishna all rolled into one. He was to appear on worldwide television and radio by June 25, 1982.[19]

Troy Lawrence, alias Darrick Evenson, claimed to be a former member of Benjamin Creme's Tara Center who became disillusioned after Maitreya did not manifest himself in 1982. He wrote a book exposing Lord Maitreya as the New Age movement's false messiah.[20] It turns out that Lawrence's story was false. He was actually an undercover Mormon who penetrated many Christian churches.[21]

Still, Benjamin Creme promotes Maitreya as the new messiah. How Maitreya will come to world power, or world religious power, is unknown. Even many New Agers do not believe Maitreya is the messiah. Although Creme has high hopes for Maitreya, there is no evidence that scares us into believing this self-proclaimed messiah will fulfill any prophetic role except Matthew 24:5: "For many will come in my name, claiming, 'I am the Christ,' and will deceive many."

Those who desire to be the messiah, like Creme's Maitreya—or even those who desire to be the antichrist, like the Satanist Faustus Scorpius[22]—will not succeed in their plans unless God permits it (Dan 11:29, 35; 2 Thess 2:6). Do not be disturbed by any reports you hear (2 Thess 2:1-2; compare Mk 13:7).

Reason 81: A Computer in Brussels Is Not the Antichrist

Every once in a while, something other than a human is elected as the antichrist. Perhaps the most widespread speculation today has to do with a gigantic computer in the European Community's headquarters in Brussels, Belgium, reportedly called "the Beast." This supercomputer is said to contain all the basic information about every human on earth. It is run by three sets of six digital units. Mary Stewart Relfe popularized this notion; it picked up steam once again with the Hyoo-go movement, which predicted the rapture on October 28, 1992.[23]

How did the rumor start? In August 1976, *Christian Life* magazine carried an article mentioning a gigantic computer that was said to take up three floors of the European Common Market's headquarters in Brussels, Belgium. The Beast, however, turned out to be a fictional creation from the novel *Behold a Pale Horse* by Joe Musser. In November 1976, Musser wrote to *Christian Life* stating:

> The item referring to a computer "Beast," a confederacy of Common Market nations, and a laser tattooing for a world-wide numbering system (People and Events, August) is based on fictional portrayals of end time events, drawing from my novel, *Behold a Pale Horse* (Zondervan), and a screenplay I wrote for the David Wilkerson film, *The Rapture*. For more than three years I have heard my story ideas circulated as fact. Perhaps, in light of what's happening in the world today, items such as the one printed seem quite plausible. However, for the moment, they are fiction.[24]

Common sense reminds us that a computer dating back to the mid-1970s would now be decades old—an outdated antique! Furthermore, it would be too difficult to maintain such a computer. How would the parts be replaced? A computer three stories high is not modern technology. Computers and their components normally get smaller as technology progresses.

Reason 82: Satan Himself Is Not the Antichrist

On the opposite extreme are those who deny that the antichrist will be a real person. According to Harold Camping, Satan is literally the antichrist. Ultimately, the church will worship Satan: "It is here that Satan will operate as the man of sin. . . . The man of sin (Satan) will take his seat (rule) in the temple (church, the body of believers) where he will be worshiped as God."[25] Camping assures us that the image of the Beast in Revelation 13:14 refers to Satan developing false gospels to deceive the church.

Though the Bible clearly identifies the antichrist as an actual man, not Satan (2 Thess 2:3; Rev 13:18),[26] Camping says that according to 1 John 4:3 the antichrist cannot be a human being, because he is a spirit.[27] But in 1 John 4:3 "the spirit of the antichrist" refers to false doctrine that denies Jesus as the Christ. It does not mean the antichrist is merely a spirit. Rather, the spirit or influence of false doctrine and lawlessness—characteristic of the coming antichrist—is already pervading the world (2 Thess 2:3-8). In Revelation 16:13 and 20:10 the antichrist is distinguished from Satan as another person (compare Rev 20:2). Both the false prophet and the antichrist are thrown into the lake of fire *before* the one-thousand-year reign of Christ (Rev 19:20-21). Then Satan is cast into the lake of fire *after* the thousand years (Rev 20:1-10). The Beast and the false prophet will already be there (20:10), and "*they* will be tormented day and night for ever and ever." The plural pronoun *they* could not be used if Satan and the antichrist were the same person.

Reason 83: There Is No Evidence That Other Candidates Are the Antichrist

I have only skimmed the surface of a vast sea of antichrist candidates. No doubt some speculate that the antichrist is Boris Yeltsin because he is from the land of Gog and Magog, or Vice President Al Gore because of his environmentalist concerns, or PLO leader Yasser Arafat because of his peace accord with Israel, or Jewish Prime Minister Yitzhak Rabin, or David Rockefeller.

If we wanted to, given all the languages in the world and the ability to use intervals of 6, 100 or what have you, we could surely dream up some way of making the name of Charles Taylor, Robert Faid, Salem Kirban or any other antichrist speculator come out to 666.[28] Any of them would find such a game highly offensive. Yet this is the very thing they do to others. Those who wrongly claim that a certain leader is the antichrist commit the sin of slander (Prov 10:18; 1 Cor 6:10-11; Eph 4:31; Tit 2:3; 3:1-2).

When will we be able to recognize the antichrist's arrival? According to 2 Thessalonians 2 and Revelation 13, we will recognize him only after a great falling away occurs in the church, after a miraculous recovery of a person or nation from a seemingly fatal wound, and after the antichrist gains world power and proclaims himself to be God to the exclusion of all other gods. Till then we shouldn't waste our time trying to figure out who he is. As biblical scholar Robert Mounce said, almost eighteen hundred "years of conjecture have not brought us any closer to an answer."[29]

12
Reasons Why
No One
<u>Has Yet Decoded</u>
<u>the Mark</u>
<u>of the Beast</u>

666 is Here!" begins a famous tract by Charles Taylor in which he shows us how our checking accounts and Sears bills contain the number 666.[1] Have you checked your Sears bill lately? Chances are the company has passed the number 666 in its account numbers by now, since Taylor's tract is well over ten years old.

Many end-time speculators occupy themselves trying to identify the mark of the Beast (see Rev 13:15-18). An array of everyday products contain the number 666. Mary Stewart Relfe shows us a brand of men's shirts in Red China that sports the number, as do the license plates of Arab-owned cars in Jerusalem. Certain shoes in Italy carry a logo with a lamb having two horns and the number 666. Some American-made floor tiles are imprinted with the number 66613.[2] We can find a good many 666s if we look hard enough. If you are concerned about the number, the next time you encounter a product displaying a 666, ask the manufacturer's representatives what they think it signifies and why it appears on their product.

The use of 666 on a product does not mean that the manufacturer is in league with the antichrist. Consider all the American Christians who, however reluctantly, have been assigned three 6s in their social security number. Does this mean they are following the Beast? Does it mean social security numbers are the mark of the Beast? Not quite.

Reason 84: All Computers and Television Sets Are Not Necessarily Involved with the Mark of the Beast

George Orwell's Big Brother is watching you! No, actually it's your TV set, according to Mary Stewart Relfe.[3] Through the use of fiber optics—threaded glass as thin as hair—the coming antichrist system may now be able to watch you through your TV or computer screen. Just think of it. While you are in the middle of watching TV or playing a game with your child on your personal computer, the antichrist could pop up on your screen and demand worship! Prophecy author Ken Klein writes: "It could be said that the basic spirit of TV, with fewer and fewer exceptions, is the Antichrist."[4] Not to be outdone, Jack Van Impe and J. R. Church calculate the number of the word *computer* at 666.[5] Are these claims for real?

Computer calculates to 666 only when one uses multiples of 6 (A=6, B=12, C=18, etc.). With such an arbitrary starting point, we could claim that the antichrist already died, because Hitler's name rings up at 666 when we start with A=100, B=101, C=102 and so forth. Furthermore, this calculation works only with the English word *computer*. In other languages it may not register at 666. If Spain becomes the head of the European Economic Community (the kingdom of the Beast, as some prophecy hypes claim), how does the Spanish word for "computer" *(máquina calculadora electrónica)*[6] total 666?

There is simply no evidence that the government can see our daily activities via fiber optics through our television and computer screens. Such notions may be plausible in a James Bond movie, but not in reality. Even if the United States has such technology, the right to privacy is still cherished by Americans and guaranteed by law.

Reason 85: The Sunday Sabbath Law Is Not the Mark of the Beast

"Of course the Catholic church claims that the change [from Saturday to Sunday] was her act . . . and the act is a *MARK OF HER AU-THORITY!*" This bizarre statement made by H. F. Thomas, a Roman Catholic chancellor to Cardinal Gibbons back in November 1895, is used by certain Seventh-day Adventist groups to show that the papacy is the Beast. Supposedly the papacy is plotting to unify all churches by the year 2000. At this time, they will enforce the Sunday Sabbath Law, which is the mark of the Beast.[7] The Latin term *Vicarius Filii Dei,* "Vicar of the Son of God," reportedly adds up to 666 using Roman numerals. In Greek, *Lateinos* (Latin man) becomes 666, and *Roman kingdom* also adds up to 666 in Hebrew.[8]

Ironically, it seems that anti-Catholics borrowed the term *Lateinos* from the church Father Irenaeus, one of the founding fathers of Roman Catholic theology! It originally stood for the Roman Empire, not the Roman Catholic Church. Moreover, *Vicarius Filii Dei* actually does not add up to 666. The Adventists added the number 5 to *u* though in their formula vowels do not receive any value. Thus this phrase only adds up to 661, not 666.

An obscure quote made by an obscure Catholic in the nineteenth century is not official Catholic dogma. Besides, the word *mark* in this context means the sign of some character, importance or distinction, not a mark placed on the right hand or forehead as described in Revelation 13. And there is no evidence that the papacy will run the world by A.D. 2000. It is silly and unbiblical to think that Christians will establish a law for the observance of Sunday and that this will somehow be the mark of the Beast.

Paul said that it is by individual conscience that each of us decides what day we wish to set aside as special (Rom 14:5). We are not to judge others in regard to the day of worship they set aside (Col 2:14-16).

Reason 86: VISA Cards Are Not the Mark of the Beast

Sometimes we are told that credit cards will herald the mark of the Beast. Jack Van Impe and J. R. Church decode *VISA* to register at 666. If we feel free to use the numeric value of a word in English, Hebrew, Aramaic, Greek, Latin, some other language or a combination of languages, this drastically increases our odds of finding 666. But even then, *VISA* does not really add up to 666. Van Impe writes: "The number '6' in Roman numerals is made up of the letters 'VI.' The ancient Greek number '6' was taken from the sixth letter of their alphabet, the letter 'sigma' which looks like the English letter 'S.' Returning to the Babylonian empire and their sexagesimal system of numbers, the programmer considered the possibility that their letter 'A' equaled 6."[9]

There is no biblical support for combining the numerical values of words in various languages to uncover some secret meaning. Moreover, the speculators can only affirm the *possibility* that *A* represents 6 in Babylonian. In other words, they do not have any hard facts supporting this speculation. It's just as possible that they are totally wrong! Additionally, they blundered in the Greek. Every beginning Greek student knows that *sigma* is not the sixth letter of the Greek alphabet—it is the eighteenth.

Reason 87: Economic Changes or New Currency May Not Usher in the Mark of the Beast

The watershed issue in the 1992 U.S. presidential race was the sagging economy. Both religious and secular sources often warn us to prepare for a coming economic crisis. Christian sources often go on to explain, however, that these economic problems will usher in a one-world government run by the antichrist, who will enforce the mark of the Beast. No one will be able to buy or sell without the mark. Salem Kirban predicts that by A.D. 2000 "people will lose their identity, become known by numbers."[10] In a newsletter promoting his book *Millennium: Peace, Promises and the Day They Take Our Money Away,* Texe Marrs predicted that this economic crash will take place in the 1990s "and quite possibly by 1993."[11] Some Christians are concerned that the United States will soon offer a new monetary system connected with the mark of the Beast. Recent changes on U.S. bills are said to foreshadow this.[12]

Should we be concerned about a new currency? James McKeever responds: "Countries frequently change their currency, sometimes drastically in size, graphics and color, without affecting anything, and both the old and the new currencies are in circulation at the same time."[13] In fact, the United States has changed its currency at least thirty times since the republic was founded.[14] Those of us who have been around a while can still remember buffalo nickels and Benjamin Franklin half-dollars. The government must change currency every now and then in the effort to combat counterfeit currency. A new currency is nothing to be alarmed about.

But let us suppose the Western world becomes a cashless society by the year 2000. Will this be a sign that the antichrist is here? No, not unless we are told to worship or swear allegiance to an antichrist. A cashless society might actually solve much of the crime problem, especially the drug trade. If our right to privacy remains, let us say amen to such a system! Credit cards, IDs, social security numbers, electronic transfer numbers and the like cannot become the mark of the Beast until the Beast appears.

Reason 88: The Current Universal Product Code Is Not the Mark of the Beast

As a young college student eager to serve the Lord, I often "witnessed" by pointing at a can of soda in someone's hand and identifying the black bars of the universal product code as the mark of the Beast. But one day a young woman simply would not buy my dogmatic affirmations that the UPC was the mark of the Beast. I was forced to change my approach, telling her about Jesus and how he could change her life. To my surprise, she responded with interest and allowed me to pray for her. That week she visited my church and accepted Christ as her Savior. Had I continued to insist that the UPC was the mark of the Beast, things might have turned out differently. Eventually I abandoned the UPC scare tactic. Thank God I did.

Figure 3. A UPC symbol.

The universal product code (see figure 3) is a favorite candidate for the mark of the Beast. The paired longer bars in the front, middle and end of the code are not secret configurations meaning the number 6 and adding up to 666. Computer bar-code expert Dong Joon Park, a distributor of the universal product code in Korea, says that the lines at the beginning, middle and end of UPC codes are simply dividers.[15] These guard bars are not numbers; they do not add up to 666. They function as the programmers for the scanner, telling it when to read and stop reading the bars. And the other bar lines are coded to numbers that appear on the bottom of the bars, so nothing is secretive about the bars.[16]

Ken Klein notes that the thin paired bars for 6 are the same width as the guard bars—hence the guard bars do function as sixes.[17] But this is misleading. All bar codes are not the same. If you pick up several products with the UPC symbol, you will notice that sometimes bar lines for the number six have varying widths. Moreover, on some UPC symbols the space between two 3s, or between a 3 and a 5 (as in the symbol above), or between a 5 and a 4, can match the space between the guard bars. All in all, spaces between the bar numbers vary in width, and most UPC codes don't add up to 666. The current UPC symbol is not the mark of the Beast.

Reason 89: The Biochip May Not Be the Mark of the Beast

Here is a more recent candidate for the mark of the Beast: a microchip the size of a grain of rice that can be implanted under the skin. The biochip, as it is called, has been effectively tested on animals. It can serve as a tag for dogs and cats, containing their name, owner's name and other important information.[18] The same chip can be implanted in a human as a type of smart card, containing the person's biography.

Could such a system be manipulated by the antichrist? Once again, there must first arise an antichrist to work the system. We have no real evidence that such a man now exists.

There is also no evidence that the biochip will be used on the entire human race. At $4.50 a chip, it could be an expensive enterprise to mark over five billion people, unless the people are forced to pay for it themselves. And such chips could easily malfunction, cause skin infections and so forth. Chip replacement would be tedious.

As technology proliferates, new inventions do not indicate how near we are to the end. People used to think that bar lines on the bottom of personal checks were the mark of the Beast, and after that they said credit cards were the mark.

If the antichrist had lived in the first century, he could have easily fulfilled Revelation 13:16-18 by ordering a tattoo or branding-iron mark placed on everyone. Such primitive means would suffice to carry out the Beast's job. Of course, computers and electronic networks would allow an antichrist today to keep tabs on everyone more easily than a first-century antichrist could have done. So inventions like the biochip give us a better explanation of how the mark of the Beast could be implemented, but they do not necessarily herald the mark of the Beast.

There is no evidence that any candidate for the mark of the Beast is in fact the mark. And none of these candidates gives us a date for the end, nor do they even show that the Beast will arise in our generation.

13
Reasons Why
No One
<u>Should Set Dates</u>
<u>for the</u>
Second Coming

*O*N THURSDAY, JUNE 9, I WILL RIP THE EVIL FROM THIS EARTH." The Lord apparently gave this prophecy through his messenger Pastor John Hinkle of Christ Church, Los Angeles. Hinkle claimed that on June 9, 1994, "the most cataclysmic event since the resurrection of Christ" would take place "on the outside" and be felt on the "inside."[1] His message was shared on the Trinity Broadcasting Network (TBN). TBN host Paul Crouch declared, "John has promised to be our special guest on June 9, 1994—that is, *if we have not already been lifted to meet the Lord in the air!*" Crouch continued, "*How we need your prayers and faithful support as never before.* . . . Dear Partners—we are almost HOME!"[2]

Date-setters can easily manipulate their followers once they get hooked on a doomsday just around the corner. Money and possessions mean little to a person convinced that Judgment Day is a few months away. And this is why many abusive practices are made easier by date-setting.

When June 9 arrived, Hinkle did not appear on *Praise the Lord*. As the midnight hour approached, the great "cataclysmic event" was reduced to Hinkle's proclamation to his congregation that some spiritual veil had been torn in the spirit realm.

Reason 90: Date-Setting Can Ruin a Believer's Faith When the Prophecy Fails

Lee Jang Rim, who was influenced by the prophetic writings of American evangelist Percy Collett, became an overnight sensation with his Korean bestseller whose title may be roughly translated *Getting Close to the End*. Published in the late 1980s, this book was the driving force behind the Hyoo-go movement, which promoted October 28, 1992 as the date for the rapture. Hyoo-go churches included Rim's Dami Church (known in the United States as Mission for the Coming Days), teenage prophet Bang Ik Ha's Taberah World Mission, the Shalom Church and Maranatha Mission Church, to name a few. Worldwide membership fluctuated between twenty thousand and one hundred thousand members.

Then the fateful day arrived. About one thousand hopefuls filled the Dami Church in Seoul on October 28 to await for the rapture. Some fifteen hundred Seoul police officers and two hundred detectives waited in and outside the church, fearing a mass suicide if the rapture did not take place. When October 29 arrived, many began to weep. One distraught member of the movement cried, "God lied to us."[3] Others attacked the preachers who had led them to believe the prophecy. Cult researcher Tahk Myung-hwan took away two knives from deprogrammed members who had intended to kill their pastors. (Tahk himself was seriously stabbed as he passed out flyers against the movement.[4])

Violence and bitterness toward God are natural results of prophecy gone astray. We should never underestimate the potential disillusionment that believers might experience when human-generated prophecies fail.

Reason 91: Date-Setting Can Ruin a Teacher's Reputation When the Prophecy Fails

R. G. Stair of Waterboro, South Carolina, broadcast his *Overcomer* radio program nationwide on nearly one hundred stations. He predicted an economic collapse in the United States in April 1988. As "God's end-time prophet to America," Stair proclaimed that a nuclear war would wipe out every major American city by the end of 1988. To prepare for the coming hardships, the self-proclaimed prophet urged followers to move out of cities into the country. And many did just that. They sold their homes and donated their money to Stair's Faith Cathedral Fellowship.

Stair readjusted his dates when doomsday didn't come as scheduled, but his supporters finally wised up. Many of the radio stations that had aired his program dropped it, and Stair fell into financial straits.[5] Another minister had lost his credibility.

Every time a preacher or teacher sets a date that fails to come to pass, he or she loses credibility among discerning believers. This unfortunate doom now awaits Harold Camping of *Open Forum,* who has already lost credibility with some of his colleagues at Family Radio.[6] Discerning Christians reject date-setters as false prophets or imbalanced teachers.

Reason 92: Date-Setting Makes a Mockery of Christianity When the Prophecy Fails

The secular media love to characterize Christian ministers as bumbling idiots who abuse and mislead their congregations. Their expectations are not disappointed by date-setters, who are covered in the media almost as much as moral and financial church scandals are. After the Hyoo-go fiasco, one newspaper sported the headline "Flash: World Didn't End Yesterday: 'We Got the Message Wrong,' Frustrated Believers Say."⁷ *The Humanist* also chalked up one more reason to mock Christianity. And a writer in *The Skeptical Inquirer* said: "If the fundamentalists are right that the Bible is inerrant, then it accurately records the words of Jesus. In such a case, Jesus would be the source of a prediction that turned out to be wrong."⁸

The Bible clearly states that in the last days, including our era, "scoffers will come, scoffing and following their own evil desires. They will say, 'Where is this "coming" he promised? Ever since our fathers died, everything goes on as it has since the beginning of creation' " (2 Pet 3:3-4). Unfortunately, today's soothsayers of the end times give unbelievers ample reason to mock Christianity. Isn't it about time we rebuked the date-setters for dragging Christ's name through the mud?

Reason 93: Date-Setting Can Turn a Person Away from Christian Faith

What happens when Harold Camping's 1994 date fails? Camping claims: "But let's suppose the worst case, that we manage to get to October, 1994, ha, ha! Camping was all wrong. What have we done in the meanwhile? We've been getting the gospel out. Is there anything wrong with that?"⁹ Yes, as a matter of fact there is. How many people will be turned off to the gospel because of Camping's false prediction? How many more unbelievers will mock Christianity? These factors will offset any good that may come as a result of his date-setting.

We often hear that many new believers have come to Christ as a result of groups' proclaiming a date for the end. But some frightening problems are overlooked amid all the rejoicing. Are such conversions genuine? How many of those who come to the faith on such a basis become disillusioned, abandon the faith or simply lose interest in Christianity once the prophecy fails? Moreover, *how many people will use failed predictions as examples of why they don't trust Christians or the Bible?* If an unbeliever hears a prophecy teacher set a date for the rapture or dogmatically claim that Russia is Gog and Magog or that the end must take place in our generation, and none of it comes to pass, the unbeliever might say: "Well, if this Christian was so sure that the Bible taught these things, and now we know they're not true, why should I believe him when he tells me Christ died for my sins?"[10]

Reason 94: Date-Setting Can Keep Believers from Planning for the Future

In October 1992 there was great social upheaval in Korea. In the city of Wonju, one group burned their furniture waiting for the rapture. In Seoul over five thousand Hyoo-go followers quit their jobs, while numerous college, high-school and elementary students played hooky. Why get an education when Christ is coming back in a few more weeks? Oddly enough, Jang Rim Lee, the Hyoo-go movement's founder, took another course. He was arrested and sentenced to two years in prison for illegal possession of foreign currency, amounting to $4.4 million dollars, swindled from naive followers. Some of his newly acquired money had been invested in bonds that would mature in May 1993![11]

Despite such negative examples, date-setters continue to profit from their prophecies. People who give up their money to such prophets often lose their future plans as well. On the radio talk show *Open Forum* in 1992, a woman asked Harold Camping about retirement planning. Camping told her, "Consider a two-year moratorium of putting money away for retirement and make as much money available as possible for the gospel."[12]

In an appeal letter dated June 1, 1993, Camping wrote:

I really believe that the urgency today to preach the Gospel is greater than ever—we could be very close to the end of time! While there is still time we must be faithful. . . . A generous gift now would be so timely. . . . Perhaps you would consider a SHORT-TERM commitment as a Faith Partner from now until the end of the year.

What should our motive be for donating money to his ministry? Camping made this clear in another appeal letter dated September 3,

1993: "But laboring in the Christian walk is of great concern and urgency—let me explain! WHAT IF THIS WAS OUR LAST YEAR TO SHARE THE GOSPEL? TIME IS RUNNING OUT!"

Some believers quit their jobs, turn down an education, refuse to plan for retirement, spend their credit cards to their limit, sell their property and surrender their finances to teachers who have predicted end-time dates. Sadly, all this is done under the guise of faithfulness to Jesus Christ.

Reason 95: Date-Setting Can Lead to Destructive Behavior

Pastor Byung Oh Ahn, leader of the Los Angeles Maranatha Mission Church, had moved to Los Angeles in 1990. His congregation, at its peak, comprised five hundred members. Due to his heretical practices, however, many members left and have formed an organization called the Federation of Victims of Maranatha. Ahn prophesied that on April 28, 1992, the door would be wide open to preach the gospel in communist North Korea. He also prophesied that on October 10, 1992, the rapture would take place. Neither prophecy came to pass.

Maranatha Mission hires security guards to protect members from loved ones who try to take their family members out of the church. In 1992 one member died of starvation after fasting forty days. The Federation of Victims of Maranatha was organized to help those whose loved ones are still involved in the sect. Former members have listed the abusive practices they experienced when they were members. They assert that Pastor Ahn claimed salvation comes through him alone and that he would give his members golden crowns in heaven once they were raptured.

Every night the members pray out loud until about 5:00 in the morning. Sometimes their throats become so sore that they begin to spit blood. Ahn's followers consider this a sign of the assurance of their salvation. Members who frequently spit out blood are the most likely candidates for the rapture![13]

One former member claims that when he attended the prayer meetings, he saw children between the ages of six and eleven participate in the "martyr training program." He says they were forced to kneel down and pray until morning. If they fell asleep, they were hit on their calves with a stick, or they had to raise their hands for an extended period of time. One former child member claimed he was forbidden to use the restroom or sleep during the all-night prayer meetings. One former minister of the group, the Reverend Tae Kwan Yook, claims that Pastor Ahn subtly claimed to be the Christ and taught that members should be willing to die for him.

Destructive behavior follows many end-times groups, whether Maranatha Mission, the Branch Davidians or the Jehovah's Witnesses. As the Hyoo-go movement raced to the October 28, 1992, rapture date, at least four suicides were linked with the movement, as well as several abortions (the women were afraid they would be too heavy to be taken up in the rapture).[14]

Evangelicals in the United States also make statements that can lead to destructive behavior. Alleging an onslaught of apostasy within almost every church in the current "final tribulation," Harold Camping writes, "There is no time left to trust your pastor or your church. You must trust only the Bible."[15] (Of course, from Camping's vantage point, "trusting only the Bible" amounts to trusting only Camping's *interpretation* of the Bible.) How can such outrageous claims be made in the name of Christianity? When believers are not rooted in the Word of God, they may not recognize that date-setting, and the abusive behavior that follows, is unbiblical.

Reason 96: Date-Setting Can Lead to Indifference Concerning Social Problems

Date-setting often makes a believer apathetic toward political and social issues. After all, why bother standing up against abortion, euthanasia, racism and poverty if the world is going to end in a few years anyway? Evangelicals have often failed when it comes to presenting a powerful social gospel. In fact, Harold Camping audaciously assumes that the social gospel is one of the signs of apostasy.[16] According to Jack Van Impe, "One who honestly feels that Christ may come at any moment is not involved with this world."[17]

This is diametrically opposed to the spirit of Jesus, who makes helping one's neighbor the criterion for one's entrance into the kingdom of God (Mt 25:31-46; compare Luke 10:25-41; 16:19-31). As James says, "Suppose a brother or sister is without clothes and daily food. If one of you says to him, 'Go, I wish you well; keep warm and well fed,' but does nothing about his physical needs, what good is it? In the same way, faith by itself, if it is not accompanied by action, is dead" (Jas 2:15-17; see also 1 Jn 4:17-18).

Reason 97: Date-Setting Can Lead to Deception When the Prophecy Fails

In the city of Smyrna (mentioned in Rev 2:8), Sabbatai Zevi fervently studied the Jewish mystical writing known as the Cabala. In 1648 he declared himself the promised Messiah and drew a large following. By 1666 almost the entire Jewish community was convinced that their Messiah had arrived. But within weeks of the new year, Turkish officials arrested Zevi.

At first disillusioned, his followers reassured each other that Zevi first needed to suffer in order to be glorified. But when the Turks attempted to convert him to Islam, Zevi consented and abandoned his messianic role for the Muslim faith. Despite this, some Jews—still believing he was the Messiah—followed him in conversion to Islam![18]

When prophecies fail, followers of end-time gurus run the risk of self-deception. Instead of admitting the failure, they would rather believe a lie. After October 1992 had passed and Christ had not returned, I spoke with Diane, a representative of the Taberah World Mission. I asked her if she still believed that her leader, Bang Ik Ha, was a prophet of God now that his prophecy had proved false. She told me Christ was "testing" his people, delaying his return to see if they would remain faithful. But no one should question Bang Ik Ha, she added, because he was the Lord's prophet.[19] Instead of accepting the truth, she justified the false prophecy.

Others cover up their errors by simply changing their dates. Colin Deal, who wrote *Christ Returns by 1988: 101 Reasons Why*, began with Christ's return in 1988, then moved it to 1989.[20] Edgar Whisenant did likewise. Charles Taylor, editor of *Bible Prophecy News*, has been suggesting and revising dates for the end since the 1970s.[21] As of this writing, Taylor's predictions are still widely respected by some evangelicals. Recently he announced that believers should prepare for a September 1994 rapture.[22]

Still, there is hope. After the October 28, 1992, rapture failed, Mission for the Coming Days apologized for its errors and disbanded. That group will never set another date for the end. We can pray that Harold Camping, Charles Taylor, Jack Van Impe and other datesetters will follow this pattern when their predictions fail.

Reason 98: Date-Setting Wastes the Believer's Time

Here is Harold Camping's ultimate challenge to his critics: "Select any year other than 1994 and then try find biblical support for that year."[23] But how can his critics rise to the challenge if Scripture forbids them to set any dates for the Lord's return? I, for one, am not willing to waste thirty years of my life calculating erroneous dates, as Camping has done.[24]

Christians can easily get sidetracked into trying to figure out the end times while neglecting personal evangelism and church ministry. Scripture calls us to make the best possible use of our time (Eph 5:16). And we are never told to calculate the date for the Lord's return.

Reason 99: No One Has Set the Right Date So Far

No prophecy regarding the date of the Lord's return has ever come true. Centuries of date-setters have all proved mistaken. Charismatic

Montanists who predicted the appearance of the New Jerusalem in the second century, Christians who believed the final century was A.D. 900-1000, Dominican monk Brother Arnold who hailed the dawning of a new era in A.D. 1260, Bohemian Father Martinek Hauska who predicted the Second Coming in 1420, German bookbinder Hans Nut who heralded the millennium in 1528, Nicholas of Cusa who predicted the end in 1734, Mother Ann Lee of the Shakers who claimed to be the incarnation of Christ in 1830—all have been wrong. From the Anabaptists' 1533 date under Melchior Hoffman, to the Adventists' 1844 date under William Miller, to the Hyoo-go movement's 1992 date under Jang Rim Lee, all dates have failed. Jack Van Impe's Great Tribulation in 1976, Arnold Murray's return of Lucifer in 1981, Edgar Whisenant's rapture in 1988 and Mary Stewart Relfe's World War III in 1989 have all proved false.

Those who follow date-setters should take a hard look at their batting average. Having played on numerous occasions for almost two thousand years, they have struck out every time. Their end-time batting average remains .000. Why? Because the Bible clearly states that no one knows the time of Christ's return (Mt 24:36; Acts 1:7).

So let God be true and every human being a liar (Rom 3:4). Let's look now at what *God* tells us we can know about the future.

14
What We
Can Know
About the Future

*A*fter reading a number of tracts and books on the end times, Gus became an avid follower of biblical prophecy. Like many new Christians, he believed the end would come in a few years. Gus was afflicted with kidney disease and a weak heart. He told me how much he looked forward to being healed at the Lord's return. Unfortunately, though, he would sometimes use the Second Coming as an excuse for not pursuing his dreams. Why bother investing in long-term goals if the Lord would return in a few short years? I explained to him that none of us has any way of knowing when Jesus will come back. Initially resisting my prodding, Gus slowly came to understand that he needed to go on with his life.

Abandoning his obsession with date-setting, Gus began to enjoy the simple things in life—a walk on a sunny day, the beauty of birds and trees—instead of focusing on his painful physical condition. And it was well that he did, for within months of my conversation with him, Gus Oropeza, my brother, died of heart failure at the age of thirty-two.

Too many Christians seem too concerned with whether they are living in the end times to realize that they have a life to live here on earth. Maybe that's why end-time date-setting is biblically bankrupt. It focuses our attention on a future date and makes us forget Scripture's warning that we are never promised tomorrow (Prov 27:1; Jas 4:14).

Date-setters ask us, "Are you ready to meet God in September of 1999?" or some other date. What the Bible asks is, "Are you ready to meet God *today?"* Death may overtake us at any moment. Tomorrow may not wait for us. Our life is but a vapor that is here today and gone tomorrow.

What Is Prophecy For?

How then should we think of prophecy? In expectation, behavior and attitude, we need to be ready to meet Christ at any moment, but we need to dream and plan as though he were not returning for a thousand years. This is the purpose of prophecy—to point us to Christ, not to particular dates; to focus our study on the kingdom of God rather than on fleeting signs of the times. When all temporary dates for the end fade into oblivion, God's appointed time for the end will still stand.

Biblical prophecy calls us to godly living, not to speculation about dates. The Old Testament prophets were primarily *forthtellers* of God's will, not merely *foretellers* of the future. They proclaimed the word of the Lord to the people, revealing to them God's intentions and will for their lives.

All too often, the prophets must show that the people of Israel have been disobedient to the Lord. Because of their sins, they will fall into a time of distress. But God promises mercy for those who repent, and he offers them hope for a future time when a remnant of Israel will experience the messianic kingdom. In Isaiah and Jeremiah, for instance, God calls Judah and Jerusalem back to his covenant instead of reliance on the protection of foreign nations. "Return, faithless people," he says; "I will cure you of backsliding" (Jer 3:22).

In the New Testament, Jesus follows in the prophetic tradition, proclaiming, "The kingdom of God is near. Repent and believe the good news!" (Mk 1:15). Jesus expects his followers to go beyond external observation of the Old Testament Law. To enter into the kingdom, true followers need to be converted and controlled by the Spirit of God (Jn 3:3-7). When Jesus speaks of his Second Coming, he mentions no date. Those who belong to him must be prepared for him *whenever* he returns, for his coming will be like that of a thief in the night (Mt 24:36-51). Those who want to be rewarded at his coming must live godly lives and bear the fruit of good works (Mt 25).

The apostles, having received Christ's teaching that he will return as a thief, encourage the church in the way of godliness (1 Thess 5:1-11; 2 Pet 3:10-12). Christians must turn away from their sinful activities and not grieve the Holy Spirit (Eph 4:30-31). They must not live in sinful "darkness," but trust in Christ and abide in the truth (Rom 13:11-14; 1 Jn 1:5-6). True believers continue in fellowship with Christ. This way they will not be ashamed when he returns (1 Jn 2:28). In the book of Revelation, Christ rebukes or commends the seven churches in Asia Minor based on their conduct rather than their knowledge of the future (Rev 2—3).

Our end-time calculations do not impress God. The aim of biblical prophecy is to transform us into a holy people actively involved in building God's kingdom.

What Can We Know About the End?

After reading this book, you may wonder whether we can know anything about the end times. Yes, Scripture does give us a few key truths regarding the end times, for God does not want us totally ignorant and unprepared (1 Thess 4:13). Here are some of the most significant things we can know about the future.

1. Jesus Christ will come again. Christ will return from the clouds with his angels and establish his kingdom. His return will be visible, and everyone, including his enemies, will see him (Mt 24:27; Acts 1:11; Rev 1:7). This has been the blessed hope of the church throughout the ages (Tit 2:13). In fact, it is one reason why the church celebrates the Lord's Supper. When we partake of Communion we "proclaim the Lord's death until he comes" (1 Cor 11:26). Although we do not know *when* he will return, we do know *that* he will return.

2. There will be a final resurrection. Both the righteous and the wicked will be raised from the dead to live forever (Jn 5:23-24; 1 Cor 15:10-58). As Christ rose from the dead, so Christians will be raised. The bodies of the righteous will have a supernatural quality, and all sickness, suffering, weeping and pain will disappear. Our new bodies, being incorruptible, will not be subject to death (Rev 21:4).

3. There will be a final judgment. When Christ returns, he will execute judgment on Satan and the antichrist with his kingdom (2 Thess 2:8-12; Jude 14-16; Rev 19). He will also reward the righteous and condemn the wicked (Jn 5:23-24; Acts 17:31; Rom 1:18). In Revelation 20—22 the lake of fire is a sign of the final destination of the wicked, and the New Jerusalem represents the final dwelling place of the righteous. Those who trust in Christ as Lord and Savior have eternal life (Jn 3:16, 36; Rom 10:9-13).

4. We are living in the last days. Here I am not contradicting what I have said earlier in this book. As many biblical scholars have pointed out (see chapter two, reason 6), we live in a paradoxical era of "now" and "not yet." The signs of the end times described in the New Testament are events occurring throughout the entire church era. So we can know that we are living in the last days, but we cannot know how long the entire last-days era will last. The final events of the last days might begin today or thousands of years from now. But as each day passes, we do know that we are one day closer to Christ's Second Coming.

Guidelines for Understanding Prophecy

Why are so many people led astray by erroneous end-time teachings? There are many reasons, but perhaps one of the main problems involves our understanding of prophecy. Unlike other portions of Scripture, prophecy probes into the future. Yet God has not chosen to reveal to us all aspects of the future. He gives us a broad, general picture of future events, and he does not intend for us to try to fill in all the details. We run into trouble when we attempt to fill in the missing pieces of the prophetic puzzle. Instead, we need to interpret prophecy in a mature and balanced manner. Here are some guidelines for doing so.

1. Avoid sensational prophetic materials. Stay away from books, manuals, magazines, tracts, charts, tapes and videos that set or suggest end-time dates or continually try to fit prophecy with today's newspaper headlines. These materials may be intriguing, but in the long run they will only disappoint the consumer. Those who claim to have discovered some "hidden" truth about the end times are almost always proved false.

2. Realize that many Old Testament prophecies were already fulfilled ages ago. For instance, if you read the entire books of Jeremiah and Lamentations, comparing them with the closing chapters of 2 Kings and 2 Chronicles, you will discover that the vast majority of Jeremiah's prophecies have already been fulfilled. They pointed to the coming destruction of Jerusalem by Nebuchadnezzar, king of Babylon. These events took place in the sixth century B.C. Biblical scholar Gordon Fee writes:

Less than 2 percent of Old Testament prophecy is messianic. Less than 5 percent specifically describes the New Covenant age. Less than 1 percent concerns events yet to come. The prophets *did* indeed announce the future. But it was usually the immediate future of Israel, Judah, and other nations surrounding that they announced, rather than *our* future. One of the keys to understanding the Prophets, therefore, is that for us to see their prophecies fulfilled, we must look back upon times which for them were still future but for us are past.[1]

3. *Realize that some portions of New Testament prophecies have also been fulfilled.* Most of the prophesied events in Matthew 24, for example, took place during the first century when the Romans invaded Jerusalem. Study helps such as a study Bible, commentary and Bible dictionary will give you access to such information. Instead of buying sensational end-time materials, invest in good scholarly tools.

4. *Realize that predictive prophecies contain symbolic language.* While some prophecies have been fulfilled in a somewhat literal sense (such as Ps 22; compare with Mt 27), other prophecies have not (for example, compare Mal 4:5-6 with Mt 11:13-15; Lk 1:17). Certain prophetic books such as Ezekiel, Daniel, Zechariah and Revelation are more symbolic than others. And numbers such as 7, 10, 12 and 40 sometimes have symbolic or theological significance.[2] The "ten days" of tribulation for the church of Smyrna, for instance, may be literal or just a way of describing a short period of testing (compare Rev 2:10 with Dan 1:12).

Some theological orientations emphasize the literal interpretation of prophecy. According to some interpretations, the rapture will occur before the Great Tribulation—understood as the final seven years of God's judgement before Christ returns and establishes his thousand-year kingdom. Another school teaches a literal millennium but expects the rapture to occur at the Second Coming. Other schools, taking a more symbolic approach to prophecy, interpret the millennium as symbolically referring to heaven or predict that the entire world will be won over to Christianity.[3]

5. *Apply sound principles of interpretation to prophecy.* These principles, commonly called *hermeneutics,* include the following.

□ Look for explanations for the prophecy in the immediate context. In Daniel 2, for example, Nebuchadnezzar's prophetic dream is not only described but also interpreted. The context is always helpful when one is interpreting Scripture.

☐ Compare Scripture with Scripture. A good study Bible or a concordance will give you some helpful cross-references. This principle is especially helpful for understanding prophecy and determining whether a passage has already been fulfilled.

☐ Look for the original intent of the author. Read the entire book you are studying and get a feel for what the author is trying to convey. Who make up his original audience? What truths is he attempting to bring them?

To help you gain a balanced perspective in your study of biblical prophecy, in the bibliography in the back of this book I have recommended some books that cover the various approaches to eschatology (study of the last things). Developing a balanced approach to prophecy will help you keep your own thinking straight and will also allow you to detect false prophecy.

When you come across false teaching, stay away from the teachers or groups. If you can, discourage others from listening to or buying materials from them. (Getting them to read this book might be a good place to start.) If you have the biblical knowledge and skill to challenge false prophets or date-setters who are damaging the body of Christ, it may be a good idea to do so.

"Be patient, then, brothers, until the Lord's coming" (Jas 5:7). Be ready to meet him. Love him and work hard till he returns, so that you may one day hear him say, "Well done, good and faithful servant!" (Mt 25:21).

Appendix: List of Reasons

Notes

Chapter 1: Fascinated by the End Times

[1] EP News Service, October 9, 1992.

[2] Russell Chandler, "Apocalypse Near?" *Los Angeles Times,* September 20, 1990.

[3] Harold Camping, *1994?* (New York: Vantage, 1992), p. 533.

[4] *Bookstore Journal,* February 1993, p. 136.

[5] *Time,* May 17, 1993, p. 13; "The Future Poll," *Beyond 2000,* special issue of *Time,* 1993, p. 13.

[6] George W. Cornell, "Scholar's Diligence Alters," *The Orange County Register,* October 17, 1992, p. E8; Russell Chandler, *Doomsday* (Ann Arbor, Mich.: Servant, 1993), pp. 45-46.

[7] We can verify these percentages by calculating the number of pages dedicated to prophecy in a modern version of the Bible. The books that are considered prophetic are all the books from Isaiah to Malachi, plus Revelation. In the New International Version of the Bible (wide reference edition, 1984), for instance, there are a total of 1,145 pages, with 269 of those pages in prophetic books. Of course this is simply a rough estimate. Not every chapter in every prophetic book can be primarily classified as prophecy; consider Lamentations 5. On the other hand, not every chapter in every nonprophetic book can be rightly classified as nonprophecy; consider Matthew 24.

[8] George Barna, *The Barna Report, 1992-1993* (Ventura, Calif.: Regal Books, 1992), p. 36.

Chapter 2: Reasons Why No One Knows the Date Through Scripture

[1] Ben Winton, "Arizona Town Fears Christmas Will Be a Day of Massacre," *The Orange County Register,* December 6, 1992, p. A36.

[2] David A. Reed, "Whither the Watchtower? An Unfolding Crisis For Jehovah's Witnesses," *Christian Research Journal,* Summer 1993, pp. 24-31.

[3] *The Truth That Leads to Eternal Life* (Brooklyn, N.Y.: Watch Tower, 1968), p. 95.

[4] Edgar C. Whisenant, *Eighty-eight Reasons Why the Rapture will Be in 1988* (Little Rock, Ark.: Author, 1988), p. 6. In Hebrews 10:25 the "Day approaching" refers to

the judgment day of the Lord, which has an immediate fulfillment (the destruction of Jerusalem in A.D. 70) *and* a long-range fulfillment (the future end-time events). Since the first century the church has believed in an impending future judgment. We are certainly approaching the final judgment and are closer to it than the first-century saints were. But this does not mean we can know the date of the end, or even that it will definitely happen in our lifetime.

[5]M. J. Agee, *Exit 2007: The Secret of Secrets Revealed* (Yorba Linda, Calif.: Archer, 1991), pp. 17-18.

[6]Some prophecies, however, tend to recur in or throughout history. So in a secondary sense these prophecies might still bear some significance in the future.

[7]Marvin Byers, *The Final Victory: The Year 2000* (Shippensburg, Penn.: Companion, 1991), pp. 7-8.

[8]Harold Camping, *1994?* (New York: Vantage, 1992), p. 534; *Talk New York,* aired October 6, 1992.

[9]Oscar Cullmann, *Christ and Time* (London: SCM, 1952), p. 145.

[10]Byers, *Final Victory,* pp. 247-52.

[11]Most scholars agree that Christ was born somewhere around 4-5 B.C., not the traditional year 1. You can study the reasons for this by consulting a standard Bible dictionary or encyclopedia under "Biblical Chronology" or the "Birth of Christ."

[12]Byers, *Final Victory,* pp. 253-55, 293.

[13]Ibid., pp. 264-66.

[14]Camping, *1994?* p. xv.

[15]Ibid., p. 444. Camping arrives at thirteen thousand years by claiming the earth was created in 11,013 B.C. He comes to this date by tracing back the genealogies of the Old Testament. But his assumptions are many, and his date amounts to nothing more than wild speculation. For a correct understanding of the genealogies, consult chapter five of this book.

[16]This event came to be called Hanukkah (dedication) and is celebrated by the Jews during the Christmas season.

[17]See Gleason Archer, *The Expositor's Bible Commentary* (Grand Rapids, Mich.: Zondervan, 1985), 7:103. For other possible interpretations, consult C. F. Keil and F. Delitzsch, *Commentary on the Old Testament* (Grand Rapids, Mich.: Eerdmans, 1976), 9:285-319.

[18]Letter to the Christian Research Institute, December 7, 1992.

[19]Jack Van Impe, *A.D. 2000: The End?* (Troy, Mich.: Jack Van Impe Ministries, 1990), audiotape.

[20]Hal Lindsey, *The 1980's: Countdown to Armageddon* (New York: Bantam Books, 1980), pp. i, 162.

[21]J. R. Church, *Hidden Prophecies in the Song of Moses* (Oklahoma City, Okla.: Prophecy Publications, 1991), p. 126.

[22]Grant Jeffrey, *Armageddon: Appointment with Destiny* (Toronto: Frontier Research Publications, 1988), pp. 171-95.

[23]Salem Kirban, *I Predict* (Huntingdon Valley, Penn.: Author, 1970), pp. 3, 21.

[24]D. A. Miller, *Watch and Be Ready! 1992 Millions Disappear?* (Stockton, Calif.: Prophetic Research Association, 1992), p. 55.

Chapter 3: Reasons Why No One Can Get Around Matthew 24:36 and Related Passages

[1]*Are You Ready for the Rapture?* (Seoul: Mission for the Coming Days, 1992), p. 73.

[2]*The Last Plan of God* (Seoul: Taberah World Mission, 1992), p. 94. The rendering of Ha's name here is as it appears in the book.

[3]Ibid., pp. 94-96.

[4]Dang Ho Cha, *The True Holy Spirit Comes from a Single Root* (San Diego, Calif.: Faithful Korean Church, 1992), p. 24.

[5]*Last Plan of God,* pp. 19, 22, 29.

[6]Harold Camping, *Open Forum,* aired September 9, 1992.

[7]R. C. H. Lenski, *The Interpretation of the Acts of the Apostles* (Minneapolis: Augsburg, 1961), p. 30; Walter Bauer, William Arndt and F. W. Gingrich, *A Greek Lexicon of the New Testament* (Chicago: University of Chicago Press, 1957), p. 824.

[8]C. F. Keil and F. Delitzsch, *Commentary on the Old Testament* (Grand Rapids, Mich.: Eerdmans, 1976), 9:495.

[9]Ron Reese, "The Midnight Hour Approaches!" (tract printed in Brooklyn, Mich.).

[10]Edgar C. Whisenant, *Eighty-eight Reasons Why the Rapture will Be in 1988* (Little Rock, Ark.: Author, 1988), p. 3.

[11]F. F. Bruce, *The Acts of the Apostles* (London: Tyndale, 1951), p. 70. This refutes Camping's outrageous claim that "not of you" in Acts 1:7 means that our date-setting comes not from ourselves, but from God! (*Are You Ready?* [New York: Vantage, 1994], p. xix).

[12]Edgar C. Whisenant, *On Borrowed Time* (Little Rock, Ark.: Author, 1988), p. 1.

[13]G. Delling in *Theological Dictionary of the New Testament,* abridged ed., ed. Gerhard Kittel and G. Friedrich, trans. Geoffrey Bromiley (Grand Rapids, Mich.: Eerdmans, 1985), p. 389.

[14]John Marsh, *The Fulness of Time* (London: Nisbet, 1952), p. 119. (The *-oi* ending of the Greek words for "times" and "dates" simply reflects that these words are plural.)

[15]On a different note, date-setter M. J. Agee claims the present tense of *knows* in Matthew 24:36 means that it does not apply to the future. Thus it is the disciples who do not know the time, not future Christians like ourselves (M. J. Agee, *Exit 2007: The Secret of Secrets Revealed* [Yorba Linda, Calif.: Archer, 1991], p. 12). Actually, *oida* is in perfect tense, not present. Granted, *oida* may *function* as a present-tense verb, but there is an important distinction between Greek and English present tenses. English tenses emphasize time, but Greek tenses emphasize *aspect*. The present function of the perfect-tense *knows* may emphasize continuous action, not time in the present to the exclusion of future time. In other words, Jesus may well be claiming that no one knows (continually, or perpetually) the day or hour of his coming.

[16]This does not mean, however, that there is never a distinction between the two Greek

words in other contexts. For a discussion regarding nuances between the two words, consult Moises Silva, *Biblical Words and Their Meaning* (Grand Rapids, Mich.: Academie Books/Zondervan, 1983), pp. 164-69.

[17]Harold Camping, *1994?* (New York: Vantage, 1992), pp. 316-18.

[18]Ironically, *ginōskō,* not *oida,* can refer to experiential knowing.

[19]Martin Hunter, *The Prophecy Book* (Jersey City, N.J.: Author, n.d.), pp. 16-17.

[20]D. A. Miller, *Forbidden Knowledge, or Is It . . .* (San Juan Capistrano, Calif.: Joy Publishing, 1991), p. 120.

[21]Those who believe that the rapture occurs after the Great Tribulation (immediately prior to the Second Coming, or simultaneously with it) are called posttribulationists. Those who believe the rapture will occur before the Great Tribulation (which they generally believe will last seven years) are called pretribulationists. Pretribulationists normally expect the antichrist to make a covenant with Israel which will start the Great Tribulation, and after three and a half years he will break the covenant. He will then persecute Jews and Christians for another three and a half years, until the Second Coming. Certain pretribulationists dogmatically claim that since Matthew 24:36 refers only to the rapture, we can know the time of the Second Coming, which will take place seven years after the rapture and three and a half years after the antichrist breaks his covenant with Israel (see, for instance, Dave Hunt, *How Close Are We?* [Eugene, Ore.: Harvest House, 1993], pp. 315-16). This position is also untenable. If the rapture occurs before the tribulation, there is still no guarantee that the tribulation must last seven years. The seven years are normally calculated from one passage (Dan 9:27) which can be interpreted in different ways (see chapter seven, reason 41, note 15).

Christian educator Philip Goodman, himself a pretribulationist, notes that even if the Great Tribulation does last seven years, no one knows when the tribulation will begin: "Will the start of Israel's seven-year-long Seventieth Week begin on the Covenant handshake agreement, at the public announcement, or will it begin with the actual signing? All in all, the whole process could take months or more. . . . Even more important, will the 1260-day countdown [three and a half years] on the term of the Great Tribulation begin when the Assyrian [antichrist] enters Jerusalem, or when he enters the Temple, or when he takes his seat in the Holy of Holies and officially declares himself to be God [2 Thess 2:3-4], or will it begin when he bans Temple sacrifices, as Daniel 9:27 implies, itself an event which could come in multiple pronouncements?" (*The Assyrian Connection* [Lafayette, La.: Prescott, 1993], p. 197).

Additionally, during the final "bowl judgments" of God (Rev 16)—toward the end of the Great Tribulation (Rev 15:1; 16:1-21), years after the rapture has already taken place according to pretribulationists—Christ reminds his saints that his Second Coming is like a thief in the night (Rev 16:15). This once again refers to the unknowability of Christ's return even during the final three and a half years.

[22]See, for instance, *Are You Ready for the Rapture?* pp. 42-45.

[23]This would be similar to Christ's refusal to use his omnipotence (all-powerful ability) when tempted by Satan to change stone into bread (Mt 4).

[24]D. A. Miller, *Watch and Be Ready! 1992 Millions Disappear?* (Stockton, Calif.: Prophetic Research Association, 1992), pp. 16-17.

Chapter 4: Reasons Why No One Can Decode a Secret Date for the Second Coming
[1]Oswald Allis, *Bible Numerics* (Chicago: Moody Press, 1944), pp. 3, 6-7, 23-24.
[2]Salty Dok, *Blessed Hope, 1996* (Pasadena, Tex.: Revelation 2:24, 1984), pp. 87-88.
[3]Harold Camping, *1994?* (New York: Vantage, 1992), pp. 446-47.
[4]Ibid., pp. 223, 438-39, 494-96.
[5]Ibid., pp. 444, 515-16, 530.
[6]Harold Camping, *The Final Tribulation* (Oakland, Calif.: Family Stations, 1988), p. 150.
[7]Camping, *1994?* pp. 235-37, 515-21.
[8]For more statistics on church growth and a balanced refutation of the sign of apostasy, see reason 33.
[9]Camping, *1994?* pp. 501, 505-6.
[10]The fact that a teacher is on TV or radio or has memorized many Scriptures or is a popular author or pastor does not necessarily mean he or she is a scholar. A genuine biblical scholar normally has an earned theological degree (preferably a Ph.D.) and more than a superficial knowledge of Greek and/or Hebrew. Few date-setters, maybe none, meet even these minimal standards.
[11]Camping, *1994?* p. 378; Stuart Holroyd, *Magic, Words and Numbers* (London: Aldus Books, 1975), pp. 90, 92; E. W. Bullinger, *The Companion Bible* (London: Oxford University Press, n.d.), appendix 10, p. 14.
[12]Rick Hall, *Why 1991?* (Las Vegas: Spirit of Prophecy Ministries, n.d.), p. 10.
[13]Camping, *1994?* pp. 504, 535.
[14]Edgar C. Whisenant, *Eighty-eight Reasons Why the Rapture will Be in 1988* (Little Rock, Ark.: Author, 1988), pp. 39-40, 44.
[15]J. R. Church, *Hidden Prophecies in the Song of Moses* (Oklahoma City, Okla.: Prophecy Publications, 1991), pp. 29, 75, 79, 91.
[16]It may be argued that specific numbers were assigned to the psalms back in the first century (see Acts 13:33). But this does not necessarily mean they were all arranged in the same order we have today. Moreover, the apostles often cite the Septuagint (the Greek Old Testament), which has a different chapter order from Psalm 10 to the end of the book.
[17]Charles Taylor, *Bible Prophecy News,* Fall 1993, p. 3.
[18]Camping, *1994?* pp. 509-11.
[19]Whisenant, *Eighty-eight Reasons,* p. 32.
[20]Cited in ibid., p. 22.
[21]Marvin Byers, *The Final Victory: The Year 2000* (Shippensburg, Penn.: Companion, 1991), pp. 327-28.
[22]Grant Jeffrey, *Armageddon: Appointment with Destiny* (Toronto: Frontier Research Publications, 1988), pp. 189-95.

[23]Revelation, Daniel, Ezekiel, Zechariah and a few portions of other prophetic books fall into the genre of apocalyptic literature.

[24]For more details on the correct interpretation of numbers and prophecy, consult the last chapter of this book. For a list of recommended reading materials, consult the bibliography.

[25]Camping, *1994?* pp. 504-5.

[26]J. J. Davis, *Biblical Numerology* (Grand Rapids, Mich.: Baker Book House, 1968), pp. 105-9.

[27]Allis, *Bible Numerics,* p. 24.

[28]Camping, *1994?* pp. 366-78, 441-43, 528.

[29]Ibid., pp. 394, 528-30. Camping's dates for Christ's birth and death are hard to reconcile with Luke 3:23, which indicates that Jesus was about thirty, not thirty-five, when baptized. Luke is very precise in his writing (see, for example, Lk 1:3-4; 2:1-3; 3:1-3; Acts 27:37). When Luke states that Jesus was "about thirty," it seems unlikely that he means "about thirty-five." At the age of thirty a Jew could enter into ministry; the Levites began their ministry in the tabernacle at this age (Num 4:47). Joseph, the son of Jacob, who is a type of Christ, started his service of saving people from a worldwide famine at the age of thirty (Gen 41:46).

[30]Jeffrey, *Armageddon,* pp. 183-85.

Chapter 5: Reasons Why No One Knows If the Millennium Will Start in A.D. 2000

[1]Margot Slade, "Forget the Apocalyspe, Woodstock 2000 Is Coming," *The New York Times,* December 26, 1993, p. 4E.

[2]Ibid.

[3]Lance Morrow, "A Cosmic Moment," *Time,* Fall 1992, p. 6.

[4]Back-cover text on Robert Van Kampen, *The Sign* (Wheaton, Ill.: Crossway Books, 1992).

[5]Russell Chandler, *Doomsday* (Ann Arbor, Mich.: Servant, 1993), pp. 47-55; Richard Lewinsohn, *Science, Prophecy and Prediction* (New York: Bell, 1961), p. 78; Stanley Grenz, *The Millennial Maze* (Downers Grove, Ill.: InterVarsity Press, 1992), p. 44. Some question the historical accuracy of reports that widespread hysteria pervaded a number of Christian communities in A.D. 999. Admittedly, it is difficult to distinguish legend from fact. Nevertheless, Chandler adequately defends the view that at least some Christians reacted hysterically at that time.

[6]Ray Brubaker, "The Unmistakable Evidence Mounts: Christ's Return Is Imminent!" in *Storming Toward Armageddon,* ed. William Terry James (Green Forest, Ark.: New Leaf, 1992), p. 68.

[7]Ron Reese, "The Midnight Hour Approaches! Your Time Is Almost Over" (tract printed in Brooklyn, Mich.; n.d.).

[8]Salem Kirban, *Guide to Survival* (Huntington Valley, Penn.: Author, 1972), p. 126.

[9]Personal communication from Bill Hoesch, public information officer for the Institute For Creation Research, March 7, 1994.

[10]For an in-depth study on genealogies, consult the *International Standard Bible Encyclopedia* (Grand Rapids, Mich.: Eerdmans, 1976), 2:1183-99.

[11]Jack Van Impe, *A.D. 2000: The End?* (Troy, Mich.: Jack Van Impe Ministries, 1990), audiotape; also Grant Jeffrey, *Armageddon: Appointment with Destiny* (Toronto: Frontier Research Publications, 1988), pp. 173-79, Martin Hunter, *The Prophecy Book* (Jersey City, N.J.: Author, n.d.).

[12]Martin Luther, *Bondage of the Will,* in *Martin Luther: Selections from His Writings,* ed. John Dillenberger (Garden City, N.Y.: Anchor Books, 1961), p. 172.

[13]Mark Noll, "Misreading the Signs of the Times," *Christianity Today,* February 6, 1987, pp. 10-11.

[14]The Epistle of Barnabas was written in the early second century A.D. The apostle Barnabas, Paul's companion, would have been dead by then.

[15]See, for instance, the ad written by Werner Goers, *Los Angeles Times,* December 30, 1992, p. B6.

[16]Alexander Roberts and James Donaldson, eds., *The Ante-Nicene Fathers* (Grand Rapids, Mich.: Eerdmans, 1981), 5:179, n. 1; Johannes Quasten, *Patrology* (Westminster, Md.: Christian Classics, 1992), 2:409; Daniel Cohen, *Waiting for the Apocalypse* (Buffalo, N.Y.: Prometheus Books, 1983), p. 47.

[17]J. N. D. Kelly, *Early Christian Doctrines* (Grand Rapids, Mich.: Eerdmans, 1979), p. 462.

[18]*Praise the Lord,* aired April 2, 1991.

[19]West Coast Prophecy Conference, hosted by Peter Lalonde and Arno Froese, November 9-12, 1993.

[20]If there is any typology derived from this passage regarding "the third day," it would point to Christ's rising on the third day (1 Cor 15:3-4).

[21]Our year 2000 is year 5761 for Orthodox Jews.

Chapter 6: Reasons Why No One Can Know the Date Through the Signs of the Times

[1]Associated Press, "Day of Doom Passes Without Quake," *Statesman Journal* (Salem, Ore.), May 4, 1993.

[2]Gordon-Michale Scallion, *The Earth Changes Report* (Westmoreland, N.H.), January 1993, p. 1.

[3]Donald B. DeYoung, *Weather and the Bible* (Grand Rapids, Mich.: Baker Book House, 1992), p. 133. Of course, this does not give us the right to pollute the air with a cavalier attitude. Global warming may not portend an impending major catastrophe paralleling doomsday; but through environmental irresponsibility we can agitate nature's equilibrium and cause minor catastrophes.

[4]Jack Van Impe, *The 90's Startling End-time Signs and Your Future* (Troy, Mich.: Jack Van Impe Ministries, n.d.), audiotape.

[5]Grant Jeffrey, *Messiah* (New York: Bantam Books, 1992), p. 141.

[6]Grant Jeffrey, *Armageddon: Appointment with Destiny* (Toronto: Frontier Research Publications, 1988), p. 202.

[7]Edgar Whisenant, *On Borrowed Time* (Nashville: World Bible Society, 1988), p. 36.

[8]Brad Sparks, "The Scandal of Nuclear Winter," *National Review,* November 15, 1985, p. 38; DeYoung, *Weather and the Bible,* pp. 142-43.

[9]DeYoung, *Weather and the Bible,* pp. 142-43.

[10]Quincy Wright, *A Study of War* (Chicago: University of Chicago Press, 1969), p. 11; Carl Olof Jonsson and Wolfgang Herbst, *The "Sign" of the Last Days—When?* (Atlanta: Commentary, 1987), p. 151.

[11]Dwight Lee, "The Doomsday Machine," *The Orange County Register,* February 9, 1992, p. J1.

[12]Johnsson and Herbst, *The "Sign" of the Last Days,* pp. 15, 22, 31.

[13]J. R. Church, *Hidden Prophecies in the Song of Moses* (Oklahoma City, Okla.: Prophecy Publications, 1991), p. 106.

[14]Noah Hutchings, appeal letter, n.d.

[15]Donald Kagan, Steven Ozment and Frank Turner, *The Western Heritage* (New York: Macmillan, 1983), 1:339.

[16]Giovanni Boccaccio, *The Decameron* (New York: Dutton, 1930), p. 5.

[17]Russell Chandler, *Doomsday* (Ann Arbor, Mich.: Servant, 1993), p. 117.

[18]Larry Wilson, *The Revelation of Jesus* (Brushton, N.Y.: Teach Services, 1992), p. 1; *Warning! Revelation Is About to Be Fulfilled* (Brushton, N.Y.: Teach Services, 1992), pp. 197-98.

[19]Albert James Dager, "Earthquake Predicted: Should We Heed the Warning?" *Media Spotlight,* July 20, 1984.

[20]Jack Van Impe, *A.D. 2000: The End?* (Troy, Mich.: Jack Van Impe Ministries, 1990), audiotape. Earlier Van Impe had claimed there were twenty-four major quakes before 1960 and fifty major quakes since then; see his *11:59 . . . and Counting!* (Troy, Mich.: Jack Van Impe Ministries, 1987), p. 27. Apparently he is not very consistent with his data.

[21]Robert W. Faid, *Gorbachev! Has the Real Antichrist Come?* (Tulsa: Victory House, 1991), p. 73.

[22]One such example is the *Information Please Almanac Atlas and Yearbook 1990* (Boston: Houghton Mifflin, 1990), which on p. 370 lists only twelve major quakes before 1950 but qualifies this by stating: "The following lists are not all-inclusive due to space limitations."

[23]Jonsson and Herbst, *The "Sign" of the Last Days,* p. 78.

[24]Ibid., p. 83.

[25]*Natural History,* December 1969, as quoted in Jonsson and Herbst, *The "Sign" of the Last Days,* p. 31.

[26]An example was Gerald Barney's "Global 2000 Revisited: What Shall We Do?" a paper that was distributed at the Parliament of World Religions in Chicago (September 1993). For a critique of the Parliament meeting, see Elliot Miller, "The Parliament of World Religions," *Christian Research Journal,* Fall 1993 (part 1) and Winter 1994 (part 2).

[27]For example: Stephen Budiansky, "The Doomsday Myths," *U.S. News & World Report,* December 13, 1993, pp. 81-91.

[28]Robert W. Pease, "Holes in the Ozone Theory," *The Orange County Register,* June 25, 1989, p. K1.

[29]Ronald Bailey, "The Hole Story," *Reason,* June 1992, pp. 25-31.

[30]Quoted in *Newsweek,* November 23, 1992, p. 56.

[31]Reginald E. Dunlop, "1994 the End!" *End Times News & Prophecy Digest,* no. 1 (n.d.): 16.

[32]Van Impe, *A.D. 2000: The End?*

[33]Bill Scanton, "Crop-Circle Hoax Claim Debated," *Rocky Mountain News,* September 15, 1991, p. 44.

[34]Gordon Stein, *Encyclopedia of Hoaxes* (Detroit: Gale Research, 1993), pp. 249-50.

[35]Harold Camping, *1994?* (New York: Vantage, 1992), pp. 54, 111, 515-16.

[36]George Barna, *The Barna Report* (Ventura, Calif.: Regal Books, 1992), pp. 32, 28, 77, 91.

[37]Ibid., p. 103.

[38]Also see Joseph Sergio, *Positive Proof* (New York: Vantage, 1994), pp. 77-80.

[39]Norval Geldenhuys, *The Gospel of Luke* (Grand Rapids, Mich.: Eerdmans, 1983), p. 442.

Chapter 7: Reasons Why No One Knows the Date Through Current World Affairs

[1]Grant Jeffrey, *Armageddon: Appointment with Destiny* (Toronto: Frontier Research Publications, 1988), pp. 113-18.

[2]Ibid., p. 101.

[3]Doug Clark, *Final Shockwaves to Armageddon* (Vail, Colo.: Doug Clark Ministries, 1982), p. 7.

[4]Special correspondent's reports, *This Week in Bible Prophecy Magazine* 1, no. 4 (1993): 9.

[5]Russell Chandler, *Doomsday* (Ann Arbor, Mich.: Servant, 1993), p. 251.

[6]M. J. Agee, *Exit 2007: The Secret of Secrets Revealed* (Yorba Linda, Calif.: Archer, 1991), pp. 258-68; summary flyer.

[7]Jack Van Impe in *Perhaps Today?* July-August 1990, p. 11; Jack Van Impe, *The 90's Startling End-time Signs and Your Future* (Troy, Mich.: Jack Van Impe Ministries, n.d.), audiotape.

[8]James T. Harmon, *The Coming Spiritual Earthquake* (Maitland, Fla.: Prophecy Countdown, 1993), pp. 84-91.

[9]Paul Boyer, *When Time Shall Be No More* (Cambridge, Mass.: Harvard University Press, 1992), p. 53.

[10]Old Testament end-time predictions commonly are connected by themes and key words rather than by a strict chronological order (for example, see Dan 7:8-27; 8:9-26; Rev 16—19). For more information about this subject consult William L. Lane, *The Gospel of Mark* (Grand Rapids, Mich.: Eerdmans, 1974), p. 449.

[11]See, for instance, William R. Kimball, *What the Bible Says About the Great Tribulation* (Phillipsburg, N.J.: Presbyterian and Reformed Publishing Co., 1983), pp. 18-50, and Gary DeMar, *Last Days Madness* (Brentwood, Tenn.: Wolgemuth & Hyatt, 1991), pp. 37-55.

[12]Adapted from Jim Stafford, "Times and Seasons," in *A Guide to Biblical Prophecy,* ed. Carl Armerding and W. Ward Gasque, 1989, published by Hendrickson Publishers, Inc., Peabody, MA 01960. Used by permission.

[13]The NIV's rendition of Matthew 24:33 and Mark 13:29, "know that it is near, right at the door," is preferred over the RSV's "know that *he* is near" (referring to Christ's return). The Greek word *estin* can mean "he," "she" or "it," but when this verse is compared to the parallel in Luke 21:31—where *it* refers to the kingdom of God—it becomes evident that *estin* here should be translated "it" instead of "he."

At any rate, even if *estin* means "he," "all these things" in Mark 13:30 cannot include the Second Coming mentioned in Mark 13:24-27. Otherwise this passage would not make sense. It would read, "When you see all these events take place, including the Second Coming, know that he is near"!

The term *generation* might also refer to the Jews as a family or clan (Walter Bauer, William Arndt and F. W. Gingrich, *A Greek-English Lexicon of the New Testament and Other Early Christian Literature* [Chicago: University of Chicago Press, 1957], p. 153), or it may refer to the wicked nonbelieving people who will continue to do wickedness even during all these signs (Mt 23:35; Phil 2:15; Rev 9:20-21). In either case Matthew 24 would then be a recurrent prophecy depicting the events of A.D. 70 that prefigure the final tribulation, where these verses find their ultimate fulfillment. Matthew 24:29 presents no problem, seeing that "those days" could refer to the entire church era, called "the last days" (1 Jn 2:18; compare Jer 31:29-34; Joel 2:29—3:2; Zech 8:23).

[14]Chandler, *Doomsday,* p. 219.

[15]Chuck Missler and Woody Young, *Countdown to Eternity: Prologue to Destiny* (San Juan Capistrano, Calif.: Joy Publishing, 1992), p. 172.

[16]Boyer, *When Time Shall Be No More,* p. 199.

[17]Jimmy DeYoung, *Ready to Rebuild* (Jerusalem: Until Productions, 1992), video; Boyer, *When Time Shall Be No More,* p. 197.

[18]Others, however, disagree regarding the interpretation of this prophecy. In Daniel 9:27, the one making a covenant with Israel is Christ, who preached the new covenant of the kingdom of God to "many" (that is, believers; compare Is 53:11-12). After three and a half years of ministry, he was "cut off," or crucified (Is 53:8). This brought the temple sacrifices to an end both in a literal sense, when the temple curtain was torn (Mt 27:51), and in a spiritual sense, by forever rendering animal sacrifices insufficient for atonement now that the Lamb of God had died on the cross (Heb 7—10; 1 Pet 1:18-19). The final three and a half years of Daniel's seventieth week, then, matches with the three and a half years of tribulation repetitively prophesied in Revelation (for example, Rev 11:2-3; 13:5). Thus the antichrist might reign three and a half years

during the tribulation, but he might *not* make a covenant with Israel three and a half years before then. For more details about how Daniel's seventieth week calculates to the time of Christ, consult reason 7 in this book.

[19]DeYoung, *Ready to Rebuild.*

[20]G. Richard Fisher, "Rebuilding the Jewish Temple: Imminent or Imaginary?" *The Quarterly Journal—Personal Freedom Outreach,* October-December 1990, p. 5.

[21]Richard N. Ostling, "Time for a New Temple?" *Time,* October 16, 1989, p. 64.

[22]Boyer, *When Time Shall Be No More,* p. 199; Thomas Ice and Randall Price, *Ready to Rebuild: The Imminent Plan to Rebuild the Last Days Temple* (Eugene, Ore.: Harvest House, 1992), pp. 264-65.

[23]David Briggs, "Prophecies of Doom Flourish As Crisis Escalates in Mideast," *The Ventura County [Calif.] Star Free Press,* February 17, 1991, p. A9. For examples of prophecy sales during the Gulf crisis, see chapter one of this book.

[24]Jeffrey L. Sheler, "A Revelation in the Middle East," *U.S. News & World Report,* November 19, 1990.

[25]See, for instance, E. H. Jim Ammerman and Charlene Ammerman, *After the Storm* (Nashville: Star Song Communications, 1991).

[26]West Coast Prophecy Conference (hosted by Peter Lalonde and Arno Froese), Irvine, Calif., November 11, 1993. See also "Red Alert! Red Alert! Peace Covenant Is Signed!!" (tract by Maranatha Ministries, Brooklyn, Mich.).

[27]Dan O'Neill and Don Wagner, *Peace or Armageddon? The Unfolding Drama of the Middle East Peace Accord* (Grand Rapids, Mich.: Zondervan, 1993), p. 96.

[28]West Coast Prophecy Conference, November 12, 1993.

[29]O'Neill and Wagner, *Peace or Armageddon?* p. 62.

[30]Quoted in Boyer, *When Time Shall Be No More,* p. 162.

[31]Ibid., p. 143.

[32]Tim LaHaye, "Will God Destroy Russia?" in *Storming Toward Armageddon: Essays in Apocalypse,* ed. William Terry James (Green Forest, Ark.: New Leaf, 1992), p. 259.

[33]William Goetz, *Apocalypse Next: Updated* (Cathedral City, Calif.: Horizon Books, 1981), p. 126.

[34]David Webber, pastor's letter, March 1980; C. S. Lovett, "Is Russia About to Invade Israel?" *Personal Christianity,* January 1981, p. 2.

[35]Jack Van Impe, "1999? Global March to Israel," *Perhaps Today,* May-June 1993, pp. 3-7.

[36]*Bible in the News,* March 1989, p. 7; Grant Jeffrey, *Messiah* (New York: Bantam Books, 1992), pp. 49, 51.

[37]James McKeever in *End-Time News Digest,* March 1989, p. 15, quoted in Boyer, *When Time Shall Be No More,* p. 177.

[38]Hilton Sutton in *Update,* February 1992, p. 9.

[39]Boyer, *When Time Shall Be No More,* p. 69.

[40]Edwin Yamauchi, *Foes from the Northern Frontier* (Grand Rapids, Mich.: Baker Book House, 1982), pp. 24-29.

[41] *The New Encyclopaedia Britannica* (Chicago: Encyclopaedia Britannica, 1988), 3:321.

[42] For insight see J. Paul Tanner, "Daniel's 'King of the North': Do We Owe Russia an Apology?" *Journal of Evangelical Theological Studies,* September 1992, pp. 322-26.

[43] Yamauchi, *Foes from the Northern Frontier,* pp. 22-23.

[44] Some say that because the Russians will have to traverse steep mountainous regions, they will need to travel on horses. Are all Russian soldiers currently being trained to ride horses for such a battle? If five-sixths of Russia will be destroyed in this war, this would amount to millions of soldiers—hence millions of horses. Will they ride these horses all the way from Russia to Palestine? If not, how will the millions of horses be transported? If by aircraft, why can't the soldiers themselves be transported by aircraft across the hills? These types of explanations raise more problems than they solve.

[45] James Risen, "What Arms Talks Were in Cold War, Trade Talks Are Now," *Los Angeles Times,* December 15, 1993, p. A18; "U.S., Europe Settle Trade Issues, Shelve Entertainment Dispute," *Los Angeles Times,* December 15, 1993, pp. A1, A18.

[46] Noah Hutchings, appeal letter received July 1993.

[47] Jack Van Impe, *The E.C. Antichrist* (Troy, Mich.: Jack Van Impe Ministries), audio-tape.

[48] Salem Kirban, *I Predict* (Huntingdon Valley, Penn.: Author, 1970), p. 21.

[49] Roy Rivenburg, "Is the End Still Near?" *Los Angeles Times,* July 30, 1992, p. E4.

[50] Apostolic Prophetic Voice, *The Next "7" Years* (special newsletter issue, Dayton, Ohio), January 17, 1993.

[51] George Eldon Ladd, *The Revelation of John* (Grand Rapids, Mich.: Eerdmans, 1972), p. 168.

[52] Alan Johnson in *The Expositor's Bible Commentary,* ed. Frank E. Gaebelein (Grand Rapids, Mich.: Zondervan, 1981), 12:515.

[53] Donald Kagan, Steven Ozment and Frank Turner, *The Western Heritage* (New York: Macmillan, 1983), 1:333-35.

[54] Samuel Bacchiocchi, "False Eschatology," *End-Times News Digest,* August 1989, p. 4.

[55] Cited from the Millennium Watch Institute's *Millennial Prophecy Report,* November 1993, pp. 33-34.

[56] James Lloyd, *Beyond Babylon: The Last Week of the World* (Ashland, Ore.: Author, 1992), pp. 100-102.

[57] Mary Stewart Relfe in *Relfe's Review,* February 1983, p. 5; *The Christian Newsletter,* June 1, 1989, p. 5.

[58] James McKeever, "Who Is Mystery Babylon?" *End Times News Digest,* April 1991, pp. 8-9.

[59] Dave Hunt, *Global Peace and the Rise of Antichrist* (Eugene, Ore.: Harvest House, 1990), p. 120.

[60] Some may object to this, claiming the church is an invisible entity. Nevertheless, the invisible church must still *visibly* congregate somewhere, and Catholic and Eastern Orthodox churches were the only places to do so. There is no evidence that any other

group claiming to be Christian existed between the first century and the Reformation. Even Protestants who are vehemently anti-Catholic will usually admit that some of the Catholic saints were probably saved—thus admitting that the visible representative of Christ had members who were also part of his invisible church. This too was promised in Scripture, that in the latter years of Christianity *some* (but not all) would depart from the faith (1 Tim 4:1).

61Bible scholar Alan Johnson notes: "The seven hills belong to the monster [Rev. 17:3], not the woman. It is the woman (i.e., the city [v. 18]) who sits upon (i.e., has mastery over) the seven heads (or seven hills) of the monster. If the woman is the city of Rome, it is obvious that she did not exercise mastery over seven successive Roman emperors that are also seven traditional hills of Rome. This introduces an unwarranted twisting of the symbolism to fit a preconceived interpretation." In *The Expositor's Bible Commentary*, 12:558.

62Kagan, Ozment and Turner, *The Western Heritage*, 1:362.

63*Mystery* in Revelation 17:5 probably does not allude to some ancient mystery religion. It simply refers to the mystery expressed in Revelation 17:7 and explained in vv. 8-18.

64Bruce Metzger, *Breaking the Code: Understanding the Book of Revelation* (Nashville: Abingdon, 1993), p. 85.

65Charles H. Dyer with Angela Elwell Hunt, *The Rise of Babylon: Sign of the End Times* (Wheaton, Ill.: Tyndale House, 1991).

66Michael Ross, "Can Babylon Relive Its Glory Days?" *Los Angeles Times*, January 16, 1987, p. A10.

67Texe Marrs, "Will You Sell Your Soul to the Devil for a Million Dollars?" *Flashpoint*, June 1993, pp. 1-2; "Chuck Colson: The Pied Piper of Ecumenicism," *Flashpoint*, October 1993, p. 2.

68Marrs, "Will You Sell Your Soul"; Charles Taylor in *Bible Prophecy News*, Summer 1993, p. 2.

69Chuck Colson, *1993 Templeton Address* (Washington, D.C.: Prison Fellowship, 1993), audiotape. Despite Colson's directness, Dave Hunt claims he did not present the true gospel because he used "vague words acceptable to all religions" and failed to warn his audience about God's judgment upon them ("Questions and Answers," *The Berean Call*, November 1993, p. 7). Using these criteria, we would have to say that when Peter preached on the Day of Pentecost (and three thousand were saved), he was not preaching the true gospel because he failed to *clearly* state that his hearers were going to hell and that Christ's death paid the penalty to satisfy the wrath of God so they could be forgiven (see Acts 2)! The apostle Paul would have also failed this test. When preaching to the pagan philosophers, Paul used terminology acceptable to adherents of local religions and even quoted pagan sources (Acts 17:22-32).

70John Zipperer, "The Elusive Quest for Religious Harmony," *Christianity Today*, October 4, 1993, pp. 42-44.

[71]George Bush, "Address to the Nation," September 16, 1990, quoted in Peter Lalonde, *One World Under Anti-Christ* (Eugene, Ore.: Harvest House, 1991), p. 20.

[72]Ed Hinson, *End Times, the Middle East and the New World Order* (Wheaton, Ill.: Victor Books, 1991), p. 14.

[73]Clyde Edminster, "Why Is There Over a Million Foreign U.N. Troops in America?" *Christ Is the Answer: A Christian Journal with an End Time Message* (Rainier, Wash.), January-February 1993, p. 6.

[74]Chandler, *Doomsday*, p. 42.

[75]Boyle, *When Time Shall Be No More*, p. 65.

[76]DeMar, *Last Days Madness*, p. 8.

Chapter 8: Reasons Why No One Knows the Date Through Modern-Day "Prophets"

[1]"A Ukrainian Cult Faces Crackdown," *The New York Times,* November 7, 1993, p. 6Y; Mary Mycio, "Ukrainians Seize Two Fugitive Cult Leaders," *Los Angeles Times,* November 12, 1993, p. A16.

[2]James Bjornstad, *Twentieth Century Prophecy* (Minneapolis: Dimension Books, 1973), p. 73.

[3]Jess Stern, *Edgar Cayce, the Sleeping Prophet* (New York: Bantam Books, 1967), p. 33; Hugh Lynn Cayce, *Earth Changes Update* (Virginia Beach, Va.: A.R.E. Press, 1980), pp. 86-99; quotation from p. 87.

[4]Bjornstad, *Twentieth Century Prophecy*, pp. 86-88.

[5]There have been reports of land resurfacing off the Bahamas, but these are only rumors. Daniel Cohen writes: "The area off the Bahamas has been explored many times by competent scientists. They have found no evidence that there ever was in that region any continental land mass or large 'lost' island or anything else that could be remotely related to Atlantis" (*Waiting for the Apocalypse* [Buffalo, N.Y.: Prometheus Books, 1983], p. 82).

[6]Mary Stewart Relfe, "Countdown to the Great Tribulation," *Relfe's Review,* February 1983, p. 4.

[7]Ibid., p. 5.

[8]Refer to chapters one and two of this book for further information.

[9]C. Douglas Weaver, *The Healer-Prophet William Marrion Branham* (Macon, Ga.: Mercer University Press, 1987), pp. 151-57.

[10]William Branham, *Footprints in the Sands of Time* (Jeffersonville, Ind.: Spoken Word Ministry, 1975), p. 74; Kurt Koch, *Occult Bandage and Deliverance* (Grand Rapids, Mich.: Kregel, 1971), pp. 49-50.

[11]Eric Pement, "William Branham: An American Legend," *Cornerstone* 15, no. 81 (1986): 14; O. A. Jorgensen, "A God Ordained Prophet," paper from Bible Believers Association, Newfoundland, n.d.

[12]Duane Dean, "The Spoken Word Is the Original Seed," in a newsletter from the Spoken Word Ministry (Barstow, Fla., n.d.), pp. 3-4.

[13]William Branham, *The Revelation of the Seven Seals* (Tucson, Ariz.: William Bran-

ham Evangelistic Association, 1967), pp. 160, 246, 291, 315, 319.

[14]Vinson Synan, *The Holiness-Pentecostal Movement in the United States* (Grand Rapids, Mich.: Eerdmans, 1971), p. 111.

[15]William Branham, *An Exposition on the Seven Church Ages* (Jeffersonville, Ind.: Spoken Word Ministry, n.d.), p. 322.

[16]William Branham, *Revelation Chapter Four #3* (Jeffersonville, Ind.: Voice of Good Recordings, 1961), audiotape.

[17]Walter Martin, *Jonestown: Death of a Cult* (San Juan Capistrano, Calif.: Christian Research Institute, n.d.), audiotape.

[18]Moses David, *The Basic Mo Letters* (Geneva, Switzerland: Children of God, 1976), p. 939.

[19]Joe Maxwell, "Children of God Revamp Image, Face Renewed Opposition," *Christian Research Journal*, Fall 1993, p. 6.

[20]Ron Rhodes, *Christian Research Newsletter* 3, no. 3 (1990): 6.

[21]*Kingdom Ministry*, May 1974, p. 3.

[22]*The Watchtower*, April 1, 1972, p. 197.

[23]*Doctrines and Covenants* 84:1-5, 31; 101:17-21.

[24]*History of the Church* 1:315; *Teachings* 17-18. Mormons sometimes object that some of these prophecies were not infallible. Nevertheless, Mormons consider Joseph Smith to be a prophet, and he made these predictions allegedly by "revelation of Jesus Christ" and "by the authority of Jesus Christ." When a Mormon leader who is considered a prophet applies such terminology to his predictions, but the predictions do not come to pass, it is self-evident that such a leader is a false prophet. For documentation and photocopies of Mormon prophecies, as well as refutations of the arguments of Mormon apologists such as Steven Robinson, write to the Christian Research Institute, Box 500, San Juan Capistrano, CA 92693-0500, U.S.A.

[25]Jeane Dixon, *My Life and Prophecies* (New York: Morrow, 1969), p. 164.

[26]Ruth Montgomery, *A Gift of Prophecy* (New York: Bantam Books, 1966), pp. 173-83; Dixon, *My Life and Prophecies*, p. 163.

[27]"Jeane Dixon and Prophecy," pamphlet (San Juan Capistrano: Christian Research Institute, 1984); Charles J. Cazeau, "Prophecy: The Search for Certainty," *The Skeptical Inquirer*, Fall 1982, p. 24; Bjornstad, *Twentieth Century Prophecy*, p. 41.

[28]Montgomery, *A Gift of Prophecy*, p. 110.

[29]Cazeau, "Prophecy," pp. 23-24.

[30]For instance, contrary to the Bible, Dixon's teachings imply that there are many paths to God (Jn 14:6; Acts 4:12). She makes use of occult objects and horoscopes, practices that are condemned in Scripture (Deut 18; Is 47:13-14).

[31]Edgar C. Whisenant, *Eighty-eight Reasons Why the Rapture Will Be in 1988* (Little Rock, Ark.: Author, 1988), pp. 34-35.

[32]Personal communication from David Bunds, December 12, 1993.

[33]Paul Boyer, "A Brief History of the End of Time," *The New Republic*, May 17, 1993, p. 30.

Chapter 9: Reasons Why No One Knows the Date Through Sources Outside the Bible

[1] *Criswell Predicts Your Next Ten Years* (New York: Grosset & Dunlap, 1971), pp. 96, 20, 23, 29, 45, repectively.

[2] *Millennial Prophecy Report* (Millennium Watch Institute), November 1993, pp. 38-39.

[3] Richard Lewinsohn, *Science, Prophecy and Prediction* (New York: Bell, 1961), pp. 80-81.

[4] *Millennial Prophecy Report* (Millennium Watch Institute), October 1993, pp. 29-31.

[5] William Alnor, *UFOs in the New Age* (Grand Rapids, Mich.: Baker Book House, 1992), p. 27.

[6] Ibid., pp. 27-28.

[7] Robert W. Faid, *Gorbachev! Has the Real Antichrist Come?* (Tulsa, Okla.: Victory House, 1991), p. 83.

[8] David Webber, "A Watch Word from Pastor Webber," February 1985; John Baskette, *Pyramidology: Key to Biblical Prophecy?* (Costa Mesa, Calif.: Answers in Action, 1992); William Alnor, *Soothsayers of the Second Advent* (Old Tappan, N.J.: Revell, 1989), pp. 37, 173-87.

[9] Reginald E. Dunlop in *End-Time News & Prophecy Digest,* no. 1 (n.d.): 12. Another popular teacher who promotes pyramid prophecy is E. Raymond Capt (*Study in Pyramidology* [Thousand Oaks, Calif.: Artisan Sales, 1986]).

[10] John W. Montgomery, *Principalities and Powers* (Minneapolis: Bethany House, 1973), p. 53.

[11] Cited from Mari Yamguchi, "Ultra-Nationalist Religion Alarms Many Japanese," *The Seattle Times/Seattle Post-Intelligencer,* October 20, 1991, p. A16.

[12] Bill Girdner, "Dispelling the Myths of Ignorance," *The Boston Globe,* May 10, 1988, p. 2. *The Man Who Saw Tomorrow* is available on Warner Brothers video (1990).

[13] Edgar Leoni, *Nostradamus and His Prophecies* (New York: Bell, 1982), p. 141.

[14] Chandler, *Doomsday,* pp. 61, 66; *The Man Who Saw Tomorrow.*

[15] Leoni, *Nostradamus and His Prophecies,* p. 169.

[16] Ibid.; Gordon Stein, *Encyclopedia of Hoaxes* (Detroit: Gale Research, 1993), p. 87.

[17] Stein, *Encyclopedia of Hoaxes,* p. 86.

[18] Chandler, *Doomsday,* p. 67.

[19] Jack Van Impe on *Praise the Lord,* aired April 21, 1994.

[20] Grant Jeffrey, *Messiah* (New York: Bantam Books, 1992), pp. 216-17, 296.

[21] Streett Meetings, Inc., " 'Vendy' Jones and the Raiders of the Lost Ashes" (1991; available from Streett Meetings, P.O. Box 724, Dallas, TX 75221). For more information about the red heifer, see reason 41.

[22] J. R. Church, *Hidden Prophecies in the Song of Moses* (Oklahoma City, Okla.: Prophecy Publications, 1991), p. 10; Jack Van Impe, *A.D. 2000: The End?* (Troy, Mich.: Jack Van Impe Ministries, 1990), audiotape.

[23] Second Enoch should not be confused with 1 Enoch, which is much older and is cited in Jude 1.

[24] Francis Johnson, *Fatima: The Great Sign* (Rockford, Ill.: Tan Books, 1980), p. 60;

quoted in Chandler, *Doomsday,* p. 206.

[25]Emmett Culligan, *Fatima Secret* (Rockford, Ill.: Tan Books, 1975), pp. 14-18.

[26]For the con position, see Michael H. Brown, *The Final Hour* (Milford, Ohio: Faith Publishing, 1992), p. 151-52; for a pro position, see Sandra L. Zimdars-Swartz, *Encountering Mary* (Princeton, N.J.: Princeton Univesity Press, 1991), p. 215.

[27]Noah Hutchings, "An Interview with Malachi Martin: 'The Gorbachev-Pope Connection,' " *The Gospel Truth,* April 1992; Jack Van Impe, *Pope John Paul: Startling Revelations* (Troy, Mich.: Jack Van Impe Ministries, 1993), video.

[28]For instance, see the prophecies of Veronica Leuken of Bayside, New York, in "Coming Events upon Man" (n.d.; available from These Last Days Ministries, P.O. Box 40, Lowell, MI 49331); and the secret of Melanie Mathieu in Culligan, *Fatima Secret,* p. 28.

[29]Culligan, *Fatima Secret,* p. 33.

[30]Elliot Miller and Ken Samples, *The Cult of the Virgin* (Grand Rapids, Mich.: Baker Book House, 1992), pp. 133-34.

Chapter 10: Reasons Why No One Knows the Date Through Rumors

[1]Rich Buhler, *The Great Christian Rumors* (Costa Mesa, Calif.: Branches Communications, 1991), p. 6.

[2]William Alnor, *Soothsayers of the Second Advent* (Old Tappan, N.J.: Revell, 1989), pp. 110-11.

[3]Jack Van Impe, *The 90's Startling End-Time Signs and Your Future* (Troy, Mich.: Jack Van Impe Ministries, n.d.), audiotape.

[4]See, for instance, Ray Brubaker in *Storming Toward Armageddon: Essays in Apocalypse,* ed. William Terry James (Green Forest, Ark.: New Leaf, 1992), pp. 62-63.

[5]Clifford Wilson, *Crash Go the Chariots* (San Diego, Calif.: Master Books, 1976), pp. 147-61.

[6]Buhler, *Great Christian Rumors,* pp. 16-17.

[7]Mary Stewart Relfe, *When Your Money Fails . . . the "666 System" Is Here* (Montgomery, Ala.: League of Prayer, 1981), p. 58.

[8]Texe Marrs, *Mystery Mark of the New Age* (Westchester, Ill.: Crossway Books, 1988), pp. 14-15.

[9]Brian Onken, "Alberto: The Truth About His Story," *Forward,* February 25, 1983 (document DR-160 available from Christian Research Institute, P.O. Box 500, San Juan Capistrano, CA 92693). CRI does not categorize the Roman Catholic Church as a cult, because its essential doctrines are in line with orthodoxy: the deity of Christ, the Trinity, the atonement and other essential doctrines outlined in the Apostles', Nicene, Chalcedon and Athanasian creeds. CRI does fault Catholicism, however, with serious errors such as papal authority, veneration of Mary and the saints, and compromising salvation by grace through faith.

[10]Personal phone conversation with Texe Marrs, September 1993; "Beware the Christian Research Institute (CRI)," *Flashpoint,* June 1994, p. 2.

[11]Texe Marrs, *Dark Majesty* (Austin, Tex.: Living Truth, 1992), pp. 100-101, 122.

[12]Walter C. Utt, "Illuminating the Illuminati," *Liberty,* May/June 1979, p. 18.

[13]G. Richard Fisher, "The Present Day Revival of the Illuminati Theory," *Journal of Pastoral Practice* 3, no. 2 (1979): 123.

[14]Ibid., pp. 124-26.

Chapter 11: Reasons Why No One Yet Knows Who Is the Antichrist

[1]Robert G. Clouse, "The Danger of Mistaken Hopes," in *A Guide To Biblical Prophecy,* ed. Carl Armerding and W. Ward Gasque (Peabody, Mass.: Hendrickson, 1989), pp. 34-35.

[2]Emmett Culligan, *Fatima Secret* (Rockford, Ill.: Tan Books, 1975), p. 33.

[3]Raymond Aguilera, *Prophecies, Visions, Occurrences and Dreams* (El Sobrante, Calif.: Author, 1990), p. 85.

[4]Ron Banuk, *Om Saleem: Prophecy in 1933* (Huntington Beach, Calif.: Author, 1993), pp. 14-19.

[5]Dave Hunt, *Global Peace and the Rise of Antichrist* (Eugene, Ore.: Harvest House, 1990), p. 5.

[6]Paul Boyer, *When Time Shall Be No More* (Cambridge, Mass.: Harvard University Press, 1992), p. 142.

[7]Ibid., p. 138; William Alnor, *Soothsayers of the Second Advent* (Old Tappan, N.J.: Revell, 1989), pp. 23, 25.

[8]Salem Kirban, *Kissinger: Man of Peace?* (Huntington Valley, Penn.: Author, 1974), p. 33.

[9]Stanley Grenz, *The Millennial Maze* (Downers Grove, Ill.: InterVarsity Press, 1992), p. 50.

[10]Russell Chandler, *Doomsday* (Ann Arbor, Mich.: Servant, 1993), pp. 42-43.

[11]Gary DeMar, *Last Days Madness* (Brentwood, Tenn.: Wolgemuth & Hyatt, 1991), p. 153. The 666 is derived by letting A-I equal 1-9, K-S equal 10-90, and T-Z equal 100-700.

[12]Boyer, *When Time Shall Be No More,* pp. 64, 65, 72.

[13]Ron Reese, "Is the Wounded Bear (Russia) Ready to Strike?" (tract printed in Brooklyn, Mich.; n.d.).

[14]Robert W. Faid, *Gorbachev! Has the Real Antichrist Come?* (Tulsa, Okla.: Victory House, 1991), pp. 7-8, 30-31, 37, 41, 47-51, 55, 178.

[15]There are no recorded vowels in the original Hebrew language. The Hebrew name for Gorbachev in Faid's book arbitrarily adds consonants to replace these vowels, while other places, when it supports Faid's point, they are left out. For instance, the first *i* in Mikhail is replaced by the Hebrew letter *yod,* but the second *i* is completely omitted in Hebrew. *Yod* also replaces all the *e* vowels in his middle name, but then the *e* in his last name is replaced by an *aleph.* These are just a few of the mistakes made in the transliteration to Hebrew.

[16]John F. Burns, "New Babylon Is Stalled by a Modern Upheaval," *The New York*

Times, October 11, 1990, p. A7.

[17]"Prophet Predicts Death of Hussein," *The Voice of Elijah,* October 1990, p. 1.

[18]Jack Van Impe, *The E.C. Antichrist* (Troy, Mich.: Jack Van Impe Ministries, 1992), cassette; Joseph Aguilar, "Juan Carlos and the New Rome," *The Gospel Truth,* Southwest Radio Church, October 1989.

[19]Tara Center ad, *Los Angeles Times,* April 25, 1982, sec. I, p. 31.

[20]Troy Lawrence, *New Age Messiah Identified: Who Is Lord Maitreya?* (Lafayette, La.: Huntington House, 1991).

[21]Book review of *New Age Messiah Identified* (document DN-037 available from Christian Research Institute, P.O. Box 500, San Juan Capistrano, CA 92693).

[22]Mary Stewart Relfe, *When Your Money Fails . . . the "666 System" Is Here* (Montgomery, Ala.: League of Prayer, 1981).

[23]Quoted from G. R. Fisher, *The Quarterly Journal* (Personal Freedom Outreach), July-September 1989, p. 8.

[24]Harold Camping, *1994?* (New York: Vantage, 1992), pp. 52, 194-95.

[25]Not all Christians agree that the antichrist (1 Jn 2; 4; 2 Jn 7), the Beast (Rev 11, 13, 17—20), and the lawless one (2 Thess 2) are all the same entity. But since Harold Camping believes this (and I happen to as well), let's assume his position for the sake of argument.

[26]Camping, *1994?* p. 190.

[27]Let's use the name Jack Van Impe as an example. Let me stress, however, that this is only an example. I do not want anyone to think Van Impe is the antichrist. When we transliterate the name Jack Van Impe into Greek—without the *J* and *V,* since these letters have no exact Greek equivalent, and keeping the *e* silent—its numerical value proves to be 222 (a=1, k=20, k=20, a=1, n=50, i=10, m=40, p=80). Multiply this by 3, since his name has three elements, and we get 666.

[28]Robert Mounce, *The Book of Revelation,* New International Commentary (Grand Rapids, Mich.: Eerdmans, 1977), p. 265.

Chapter 12: Reasons Why No One Has Yet Decoded the Mark of the Beast

[1]Charles Taylor, "666 Is Here!" (tract; Huntington Beach, Calif.: Today in Bible Prophecy, n.d.).

[2]Mary Stewart Relfe, *When Your Money Fails . . . the "666 System" Is Here* (Montgomery, Ala.: League of Prayer, 1981), pp. 17-31.

[3]Ibid., pp. 117-26.

[4]Kenneth Klein, *The False Prophet* (Eugene, Ore.: Winterhaven, 1992), p. 164; David Webber, *The Image of the Ages* (Lafayette, La.: Huntington House, 1991), p. 34.

[5]Jack Van Impe, *11:59 . . . and Counting!* (Troy, Mich.: Jack Van Impe Ministries, 1987), p. 105.

[6]Latin Americans normally translate *computer* as *computadora,* but Spaniards translate it the way I have written it.

[7]Roy Allan Anderson, *The New Age Movement and the Illuminati 666* (New Port

Richey, Fla.: Light Book Distributors, 1983), pp. 269-76; Marvin Moore, *The Crisis of the End Time* (Boise, Idaho: Pacific, 1992), pp. 99-111; *World Warning,* special issue of *The Advent Remnant Review and Sabbath Herald* (Lincoln City, Ore.), n.d., p. 4.

⁸H. D. Shafer, *The Antichrist* (N.p.: Blessed Hope Evangelical Association, 1981); *World Warning,* p. 4.

⁹Van Impe, *11:59,* pp. 106-7.

¹⁰Salem Kirban, *I Predict* (Huntington Valley, Penn.: Author, n.d.), p. 19.

¹¹Texe Marrs, "Millennium: The Day They Take Our Money Away," *Flashpoint,* October 1990, p. 1.

¹²Norman Franz, "The New U.S. Currency: Is It Anti-Counterfeit or Anti-Christ?" *Denver Christian News,* March 1993, p. 15.

¹³James McKeever, "Peace and the New U.S. Currency," *End-Times News Digest,* July 1990, p. 3.

¹⁴William Alnor, *Soothsayers of the Second Advent* (Old Tappan, N.J.: Revell, 1989), p. 79.

¹⁵Hyuk Jin Noh and Jin Young Choi on *PD Soo-Chu* (a Korean program), aired in Korea, July 1992.

¹⁶The FGH letters below certain bars, according to some end-time speculators, allegedly stand for "hand" and "forehead," as long as we toss out the *G!* Actually, these numbers appear to be alphabetical sequences such as ABC, CDE and FGH. At any rate, many product codes do not even contain such letters.

¹⁷Klein, *False Prophet,* pp. 182-84.

¹⁸Patti Lalonde, ed., "This Week in Bible Prophecy," *The Christian World Report,* October 1993, p. 7; Frank Allnutt, "The Future's 'Fool Proof' ID systems Being Implemented Today," *Colorado Christian News,* April 1993, p. 21.

Chapter 13: Reasons Why No One Should Set Dates for the Second Coming

¹John Hinkle, *Praise the Lord,* aired January 25, 1994; excerpt from a message preached at his church, June 5, 1994.

²Paul Crouch, "Send Us Around the World," *Praise the Lord,* August 1993, p. 2.

³Reuters, "Korean Sect Stunned As 'Rapture' Doesn't Come," *The Orange County Register,* October 29, 1992, p. A21.

⁴Teresa Watanabe, " 'Rapture' Movement Rocks S. Korea," *Los Angeles Times,* September 28, 1992, p. A14; "Worshipers Attack Ministers in Doomsday Debacle," *Rocky Mountain News,* October 30, 1992, p. 32.

⁵"South Carolina Prophet of Doom Attracts Widening Audiences," *Christian Research Journal,* Summer 1988; "Stillborn Infant Death Devastates South Carolina Doomsday Group," *Christian Research Journal,* Fall 1988. (As documents DS-475 and DS-477, these articles are available from Christian Research Institute, P.O. Box 500, San Juan Capistrano, CA 92693).

⁶Perrucci Ferraiuolo, "Could '1994' Be the End of Family Radio?" *Christian Research*

Journal, Summer 1993, pp. 5-6.

[7]*Rocky Mountain News Wire Services,* October 29, 1992, p. 3.

[8]Terry Tremaine, "Global Fortune-Telling and Bible Prophecy," *The Skeptical Inquirer,* Winter 1994, p. 168.

[9]Harold Camping in *New Life Digest,* no. 4 (1992): 29.

[10]I am indebted to Gary DeMar for presenting this argument in his interview on eschatology on *Talk New York,* aired October 28, 1992.

[11]"Seoul Sect Leader Gets Two Years for Fraud," *Los Angeles Times,* December 5, 1992, p. A22.

[12]*Open Forum,* aired October 1, 1992.

[13]I compiled information on the Hyoo-go movement and Maranatha Mission through a number of interviews with members of the Hyoo-go movement, nonmembers and former members, and through Korean news items translated by an individual who wishes to remain anonymous. I was not allowed to enter the Maranatha Mission Church for interviews. Nevertheless, I did manage to conduct several phone conversations with a man who called himself Na Huhn, a spokesperson for the church. He denied the child abuse and suicide charges but affirmed Ahn's prophecies and the all-night prayer meetings with blood-spitting. This phenomenon, he claimed, was a way of purging oneself from sin.

[14]*EP News Service,* November 6, 1992, p. 5; Teresa Watanabe, "No Doomsday 'Rapture' Lifts S. Korean Sect," *Los Angeles Times,* October 29, 1992, pp. A-4, A10.

[15]Harold Camping, *1994?* (New York: Vantage, 1992), p. 534.

[16]Ibid., pp. 143-52.

[17]Cited in Paul Boyer, *When Time Shall Be No More* (Cambridge, Mass.: Harvard University Press, 1992), p. 298.

[18]Leon Festinger, Henry Riecken and Stanley Schachter, *When Prophecy Fails* (New York: Harper/Torchbooks, 1964), pp. 8-12.

[19]Interview, November 1992.

[20]William Alnor, *Soothsayers of the Second Advent* (Old Tappan, N.J.: Revell, 1989), p. 38.

[21]Ibid., pp. 136-39.

[22]Charles Taylor in *Bible Prophecy News,* Fall 1993, p. 3.

[23]Camping, *1994?* p. 483.

[24]Nevertheless, I have answered this challenge by creating a mock date of A.D. 2444, using the same types of mathematical calculations Camping employs. To obtain this refutation, write to the Christian Research Institute (P.O. Box 500, San Juan Capistrano, CA 92693) and ask for my paper "The Late Great Credibility of Harold Camping."

Chapter 14: What We *Can* Know About the Future

[1]Gordon Fee and Douglas Stuart, *How to Read the Bible For All Its Worth* (Grand Rapids, Mich.: Academie/Zondervan, 1982), p. 150.

²This does not mean, however, that such numbers *always* contain a symbolic or theological meaning. In fact, very few numbers apart from 7 have any more or less consistent symbolic or theological meaning. John J. Davis writes: "The only number used symbolically in the Scripture to any degree with *discernible significance* is the number seven. It should be pointed out that nowhere in Scripture is any number given any specific theological or mystical meaning! This appears to be rather strange if all numbers such as 1, 2, 3, 4, 5, 10, 12, 40, etc. are really symbols. It is a well-known fact that, generally, when the Bible employs a symbol, it either explains the significance of that symbol in the immediate context (e.g., the candlestick and stars of Revelation) or in some other part of the Scripture" (*Biblical Numerology* [Grand Rapids, Mich.: Baker Book House, 1968], p. 119).

³The four schools I have mentioned (from first to last) are dispensationalism, historic premillennialism, amillennialism and postmillennialism. To find good overviews of these various interpretations, consult the bibliography in the back of this book.

Bibliography

Here is a list of recommended books for those who wish to pursue the doctrine of eschatology (study of the last things). These books can be either ordered at Christian bookstores or found at a Christian college or seminary library.

Dispensationalists believe the rapture will take place before the Great Tribulation that lasts seven years (pretribulation). This is followed by a literal thousand-year millennium on earth. *Historic premillennialists* believe the rapture occurs after the tribulation period (posttribulation). Christ will then establish his kingdom and reign here on earth during the millennium. *Postmillennialists* believe the world will become Christianized prior to the return of Christ. The millennium takes place when the world has generally become Christian. *Amillennialists* normally believe the millennium refers to the current status of believers in heaven. Some believe the kingdom of God is already fully established on earth.

* = *beginning level*

Books Giving an Overview of the Various Eschatological Positions

Archer, Gleason, Paul Feinberg, Douglas Moo and Richard Reiter. *The Rapture: Pre-, Mid- or Post-Tribulational?* Grand Rapids, Mich.: Academie/Zondervan, 1984.

Clouse, Robert G., ed. *The Meaning of the Millennium: Four Views.* Downers Grove, Ill.: InterVarsity Press, 1977.

Erickson, Millard J. *Contemporary Options in Eschatology.* Grand Rapids, Mich.: Baker Book House, 1977.

Grenz, Stanley J. *The Millennial Maze.* Downers Grove, Ill.: InterVarsity Press, 1992.

* Lightner, Robert P. *The Last Days Handbook.* Nashville: Thomas Nelson, 1990.

Dispensational Perspective

Pentecost, Dwight J. *Things to Come: A Study in Biblical Eschatology.* Grand Rapids, Mich.: Zondervan, 1958.

* Ryrie, Charles C. *Dispensationalism Today.* Chicago: Moody Press, 1965.

Saucy, Robert L. *The Case for Progressive Dispensationalism.* Grand Rapids, Mich.: Zondervan, 1993.

Premillennial Perspective

Gundry, Robert. *The Church and the Tribulation.* Grand Rapids, Mich.: Zondervan, 1973.

* Ladd, George Eldon. *The Blessed Hope.* Grand Rapids, Mich.: Eerdmans, 1956.

Payne, J. Barton. *Encyclopedia of Prophecy.* Grand Rapids, Mich.: Eerdmans, 1980.

Postmillennial Perspective

Boettner, Loraine. *The Millennium.* Rev. ed. Westminster, Penn.: Presbyterian & Reformed, 1984.

Davis, John Jefferson. *Christ's Victorious Kingdom: Postmillennial-*

ism Reconsidered. Grand Rapids, Mich.: Baker Book House, 1986.

Amillennial Perspective

* Hoekema, Anthony. *The Bible and the Future.* Grand Rapids, Mich.: Eerdmans, 1979.

Hughes, Philip E. *Interpreting Prophecy.* Grand Rapids, Mich.: Eerdmans, 1976.

Interpreting Prophecy

* Armerding, Carl, and W. Ward Gasque, eds. *A Guide to Biblical Prophecy.* Peabody, Mass.: Hendrickson, 1989.
* Green, Joel. *How to Read Prophecy.* Downers Grove, Ill.: InterVarsity Press, 1984.
* Kaiser, Walter C. *Back Toward the Future.* Grand Rapids, Mich.: Baker Book House, 1989.

Morris, Leon. *Apocalyptic.* Grand Rapids, Mich.: Eerdmans, 1985.

Witherington, Ben. *Jesus, Paul and the End of the World.* Downers Grove, Ill.: InterVarsity Press, 1992.

Prophecy Commentaries

* Chilton, David. *The Days of Vengeance: An Exposition of the Book of Revelation.* Ft. Worth, Tex.: Dominion, 1986.
* Ladd, George Eldon. *A Commentary on the Revelation of John.* Grand Rapids, Mich.: Eerdmans, 1972.

Lenski, R. C. H. *The Interpretation of St. John's Revelation.* Minneapolis: Augsburg, 1943.

* Metzger, Bruce. *Breaking the Code: Understanding the Book of Revelation.* Grand Rapids, Mich.: Baker Book House, 1993.
* Mickelsen, A. Berkeley. *Daniel and Revelation: Riddles or Realities?* Nashville: Thomas Nelson, 1984.
* Mounce, Robert, M. *New International Commentary on the New Testament.* Grand Rapids, Mich.: Eerdmans, 1977.

————. *What Are We Waiting For?* Grand Rapids, Mich.: Eerdmans, 1992.

Wainwright, Arthur. *Mysterious Apocalypse: Interpreting the Book of Revelation.* Nashville: Abingdon, 1993.

Critiques of End-Times Madness

* Alnor, William. *Soothsayers of the Second Advent.* Ventura, Calif.: Regal Books, 1989.

* Chandler, Russell. *Doomsday.* Ann Arbor, Mich.: Servant, 1993.

* DeMar, Gary. *Last Days Madness.* Brentwood, Tenn.: Wolgemuth & Hyatt, 1991.

Name and Subject Index

Scripture Index